The Noodle *Cookbook*

The
Noodle
Cookbook

Quick and easy recipes from
around the world

Judy Ridgway

VERMILION
LONDON

First published 1994

1 3 5 7 9 8 6 4 2

Text copyright © Judy Ridgway 1994

Photography copyright © Random House UK Ltd and National Magazine
Company Ltd 1994

First published in the United Kingdom by Vermilion
an imprint of Ebury Press
Random House
20 Vauxhall Bridge Road
London SW1V 2SA

Random House Australia (Pty) Ltd
20 Alfred Street, Milsons Point, Sydney
New South Wales 2061, Australia

Random House New Zealand Ltd
18 Poland Road, Glenfield,
Auckland 10, New Zealand

Random House South Africa (Pty) Ltd
PO Box 337, Bergvlei, South Africa

Random House UK Ltd Registered No. 945009

A CIP record for this book is available from the British Library

ISBN 0 09 179124 3

Designed and typeset by Behram Kapadia

Photography by Stephen Baxter, Laurie Evans, Graham Kirk and
James Murphy

Printed and bound in Great Britain by Mackays of Chatham Plc, Kent

Papers used by Ebury Press are natural, recyclable products made
from wood grown in sustainable forests.

CONTENTS

INTRODUCTION

Noodles must be one of the original convenience foods. They take up very little space and they can be stored indefinitely. Yet when they are cooked they expand into a filling base for healthy and nutritious meals.

Noodles originated somewhere in Asia, but the inspiration for the recipes in this book comes from around the world. Ideas from Italy, Hungary and China rub shoulders with others from California, Thailand and Japan, not to mention France, Texas and the Middle East. Once started it was difficult to know when to stop.

Versatility and speed are the catchwords for noodles. You really can serve almost any type of noodle with any topping. This means that you do not have to do a heavy shop or have a vast amount of food on hand to make an astonishing range of interesting meals. Nor do you have to have an up to the minute kitchen filled with gadgets.

All the recipes can be cooked on a maximum of two burners with a minimum of equipment. Whether you live in a bedsitter, a studio flat, a caravan or a house with a fully fitted kitchen, you will have no difficulty in making any of the dishes.

With the exception of two or three of the baked noodle dishes, all the recipes can be prepared and cooked in half an hour. If you have even less time, turn to the 'Double Quick' recipes on pages 35–50. These can be prepared in 10-15 minutes.

You can serve noodles at almost any time of the day or night. In China you might even get them for breakfast. With the recipes in this book you will find something for every occasion from snack meals and quick lunches to full-blown dinners. In fact noodles are just as useful when you are entertaining friends as when you are cooking for yourself. All the recipes given here are for two people but they can be halved or doubled up with ease.

Noodles fit well into the current healthy eating guidelines, too. They are pure starch or carbohydrate and this is the kind of food everyone is being urged to eat in larger quantities. Calories are much the same as for other starchy foods so, provided that you go easy on the fat content of the toppings, noodles will not make you fat. Indeed the toppings can be as versatile as the noodles. Vegetarians, demi-vegetarians and meat-eaters will all find something to their taste.

Noodles are easy to find in the shops. Supermarkets stock a good selection of different brands; specialist and health food shops offer an even wider choice. All these noodles vary in taste and texture. Some swell to a couple of times their original size, others expand very much more than that. There are wheat-based noodles, buckwheat noodles, rice noodles and even beanflour noodles. Some are made with eggs and others flavoured with spinach, chilli or herbs.

Because of the variety it is very important to check the cooking instructions given on the packs. Some noodles only need to be soaked in boiling water for a few minutes, while others need a longer cooking time in boiling water. They are all different – but they are all fun!

OODLES OF NOODLES

You can buy noodles almost everywhere. They are on sale in supermarkets – probably among the ethnic Thai, Chinese or Italian food – in small grocers or specialist food shops and in 24-hour stores.

The range is enormous with rice, potatoes, buckwheat, wheat and eggs all contributing to the choice. Noodles may be packed in small nests, spiral skeins or in long bundles, or they may be compressed into curly blocks.

Here is a round-up of all the types of noodles I have found so far.

DRIED EGG NOODLES

These come mainly from China or from Italy.

Chinese Egg Noodles or Stir-fry Noodles

Long round noodles which are suitable for very many of the recipes in this book. They are sometimes packed in nests or bundles.

Thread Egg Noodles

Very thin noodles which are particularly suitable for Chow Mein and Singapore Noodles and for use in soups. They may be round or flat.

Standard preparation for oriental dried egg noodles:
Plunge the noodles into a large pan of boiling water and remove from the heat. Leave to stand for 4-6 minutes. Drain and use at once or toss in a little oil and keep on one side until required.

Some brands are ready to eat after standing for 2-3 minutes. Others need to be cooked in boiling water for as long as 10 minutes. So you should always check the instructions on the pack very carefully before starting a recipe.

Italian Dried Egg Noodles
Long flat noodles which are particularly versatile. They are are often packed in nests or bundles.

Standard preparation for Italian egg noodles:
Gradually plunge the noodles into a large pan of boiling salted water, taking care to keep the water on the boil. Continue to cook uncovered over a medium heat for 8-12 minutes or for the length of time given on the pack until the noodles are just tender. Drain and use at once.

PLAIN DRIED WHEAT NOODLES
These may come from China, Japan, Thailand or Italy.

Pre-Steamed Mie/Thai Noodles/Stir-fry Noodles
Thin dry noodles which look very similar to egg noodles. They may be packed in nests or bundles. They can be interchanged with dried egg noodles in all recipes.

Dried Chilli Noodles
Long thin noodles flavoured with chilli pepper. They have quite a hot flavour and can be used in most dishes if you like a strongly piquant taste.

Dried Spinach Noodles
Long flat noodles flavoured with spinach. There are both Chinese and Italian versions on the market.

Italian Dried Flat Noodles
These include long flat pasta, such as tagliatelle and fettucine. They may be packed in lengths or bundles.

Tom Yum Noodles
These Thai noodles are packed with a seasoning mix which can be used separately to make quick stocks or soups. The noodles can be used in just the same way as egg noodles.

Three-Minute Noodles
Quick-cooking noodles which are also packed with a seasoning mix.

Japanese Somen Noodles
Very thin long noodles which thicken up quite considerably on cooking. Use in any of the dried noodle recipes.

Japanese Kintobi Noodles
Very thin flat noodles which also thicken on cooking. Use in any of the dried noodle recipes.

Japanese Wholewheat Noodles or Ramen
Curly compressed noodles which often come with a soup mix.

Standard preparation for dried plain wheat noodles:
Gradually plunge the noodles into a large pan of boiling salted water, taking care to keep the water on the boil. Continue to cook uncovered over a medium heat for 3-20 minutes, depending on the instructions given on the pack. Drain and use at once.

FRESH WHEAT NOODLES
These are fresh Italian noodles such as tagliatelle and fettucine.

Standard preparation for fresh wheat noodles:
Gradually plunge the noodles into a large pan of boiling salted water, taking care to keep the water on the boil. Continue cooking, uncovered, over a medium heat for 2-3 minutes until just tender to the bite (*al dente*). Drain and use at once.

BUCKWHEAT NOODLES
These come mainly, but not always, from Japan. They can be used in most recipes in place of egg or wheat noodles.

Japanese Soba Noodles
These are usually made with a mixture of buckwheat and wheat flour and are therefore not suitable for people with wheat or gluten allergies. They are long and thin and thicken up considerably on cooking.

Japanese Buckwheat Ramen
These too are usually a mixture of buckwheat and flour. They are compressed into a curly mass and come with a soup mix.

Standard preparation for buckwheat noodles:
Plunge the noodles into a large pan of boiling water. Continue to cook, uncovered, over a medium heat for 3-15 minutes, depending on the instructions on the pack. Some of the quicker-cook varieties will continue to expand if they are left to stand in the cooking water. Drain and use at once.

CLEAR RICE NOODLES
Originally from China, rice noodles are now manufactured here and in the US for people who are unable to eat wheat products. They can be used in most of the recipes in this book.

Rice Thread Noodles/Vermicelli/Rice Sticks
Very, very thin long noodles which are packed in bundles and are sometimes quite difficult to separate. Their main use is in soups, but they can also be deep fried and used to add interest to main dishes and salads.

Pad Thai Noodles
Packed with a soup mix which can be used separately to make soups and stocks.

Rice Noodles
These look like transparent tagliatelle or flat wheat noodles and can be used in very much the same way. They can also be deep fried to make a wonderful crispy base for stir-fried toppings.

Standard preparation for rice noodles and vermicelli:
Gradually plunge the noodles into a large pan of boiling salted water and cook for 2-3 minutes or for the length of time given on the pack. Drain and use in soups or stir-fries. Some brands suggest soaking the noodles in water for 15-20 minutes before stir-frying, so check the labels.

BROWN RICE NOODLES OR RAMEN
Japanese curly compressed noodles with soup mix.

POTATO BASED NOODLES

Some noodles are made from potato flour and potato starch.

CRISPY NOODLES

These little packets of crispy noodles are designed to be deep fried and served as a topping for egg noodle dishes.

SAI FUN JAPANESE NOODLES

Long thin rice noodles for deep frying.

CELLOPHANE NOODLES

These are also known as bean threads or glass noodles and they are made from ground mung bean flour. They are usually tightly packed into small bundles. They are only available in a few specialist Chinese grocers.

STORE
CUPBOARD

A well stocked store cupboard is extremely useful when you want to produce interesting meals in a hurry. I am a great collector of bits and pieces and I cannot enter a delicatessen or specialist grocer without coming out with at least one store cupboard item. My latest foray resulted in a jar of Chinese sweet chilli sauce, some fresh coriander purée and a pack of dried coconut milk.

Indeed cooking has become a great deal easier with the advent of fresh chopped or puréed ingredients such as herbs, green peppers, lemon grass, ginger and garlic preserved in oil. You no longer have to scour the high street to find all the fresh flavours given in a recipe.

Here is a list of some of the items you might consider keeping on hand. The final choice will depend upon your own personal preferences and the size of your storage area.

Basics:
Stock cubes: beef, chicken, vegetable and fish
Canned beans and baked beans
Canned tomatoes
Tomato purée
Dried or frozen herbs or chopped herbs in oil
Grated root ginger in oil
Olives
Sesame oil
Selection stir-fry sauces
Soy sauce
Tabasco sauce
Mayonnaise

Exotics:
Lemon grass in oil
Dried coconut milk
Dried wild mushrooms

Sun-dried tomatoes
Selection of vegetables pastes: olive, artichoke, pimento
Italian pesto sauce
Capers
Sweet chilli sauce and barbecue sauces
Canned Chinese vegetables: beansprouts, bamboos shoots, Water chestnuts

If you have a freezer, the latest offering is a wonderful range of frozen chopped herbs. All you have to do is shake them out of the bag straight from the freezer. There are nine different herbs on offer, together with three herb mixes, garlic and shallots. They are not too expensive and have the advantage of keeping for quite a long time.

NOODLE
SOUPS

There is nothing like a really good noodle soup to quench all pangs of hunger. It is a meal in itself. Simply add more or less noodles depending on how filling you want the soup to be. Japanese, Thai and Chinese cooks have always had a very thin dividing line between what constitutes a soup and what is a dish with a very runny sauce and my recipes follow in that tradition.

I have put together twelve recipes for this section, but the scope is endless. Very often the inspiration for a soup comes from the items I happen to have in the fridge or store cupboard and there is no reason why you should not do the same with whatever you have to hand.

However, you do need a good strong stock base to start with. Some supermarkets sell cartons of ready-made stock. If you cannot find these you can make stock quite quickly by using a good brand of stock cube, perhaps mixed with a meat or yeast extract.

Allow 1 stock cube to 450ml/¾ pint water for a strong stock. Vary this according to the recipe or your own taste. Alternatively, dissolve 1 beef or vegetable stock cube with 1 level teaspoon of Bovril or Marmite in 600ml/1 pint boiling water.

Some packs of noodles, particularly those for Thai or Japanese dishes, come with a spice or flavouring pack and these too can be used on their own with water or with other stock mixes.

Any kind of noodles can be used in soup. Thin vermicelli or thread noodles are traditional to both East and West but don't let that stop you using whatever noodles you happen to have in your store cupboard.

The noodles are best added to soup with just sufficient time left for them to cook through. Both dried noodles and fresh pasta noodles soak up more and more liquid if left to stand for any length of time and this could turn your runny soup into a thicker mass. This is easily solved by adding more stock.

Quick Chicken Noodle Soup

This is a really quick soup to make and it is also very versatile. You can use any kind of thin noodles; wheat, buckwheat or rice. This recipe is thoroughly Western in flavour but it is quite easy to give it an Eastern feel by adding a teaspoon or two of soy or tamari sauce, a Mexican slant by adding Tabasco, or a Thai flavour by adding lemon grass and coriander.

600ml / 1 pint chicken stock made with 1½ chicken stock cubes and boiling water

1 cooked chicken joint

1 small courgette or 1 small leek, trimmed and sliced

2 tablespoons fresh or frozen peas

2 tablespoon sweetcorn kernels

40-50g / 1½-2oz thread or vermicelli noodles

salt and freshly ground black pepper

1. Pour the stock and into a saucepan and bring to the boil.

2. Remove the meat from the chicken joint discarding the skin and bones. Cut into strips and add to the stock in the pan.

3. Add the vegetables to the pan and return to the boil. Reduce the heat and simmer for 5-6 minutes. Check that the pieces of chicken are cooked through.

4. Add the noodles and seasoning and cook or stand for the length of time given on the pack.

Variation
* Add any kind of quick-cook or stir-fry vegetables which are to hand.

Beefy
Noodle Soup

This simple noodle soup can be expanded into a filling main course soup by adding more vegetables and increasing the quantity of noodles. Shredded cold beef gives a really sumptuous touch.

**450ml / ¾ pint strong beef stock made with
1 beef stock cube and boiling water**

1 carrot

**4-6 spring onions, trimmed and sliced lengthways,
or ½ small onion, peeled and sliced**

40g / 1½oz dried egg noodles

salt and freshly ground black pepper

2 tablespoons freshly chopped parsley

1. Pour the stock into a saucepan and bring to the boil. Reduce the heat and simmer gently.

2. Peel the carrot and discard the peel. Then continue to peel off thin layers of carrot with the potato peeler and add to the stock. Add the spring onion or onion and return to the boil. Cook for 2 minutes.

3. Add the dried egg noodles and seasoning and cook or stand for the length of time given on the pack.

4. Spoon into soup bowls and garnish with freshly chopped parsley.

Variations

* Add 2 tablespoons cooked red kidney beans and a dash of Tabasco sauce in winter or use chilli flavoured noodles.

* Add 2 tablespoons sweetcorn kernels and diced tomatoes in summer.

Oriental Seafood Soup

This very quick and easy-to-make soup not only looks very attractive but is also filling enough to make a good main course. The hungrier you are the more noodles you should add!

2 small fillets of lemon sole, skinned

450ml / ¾ pint ready-made fish stock or 2 fish stock cubes dissolved in 450ml / ¾ pint boiling water

1 x 5mm / ¼ in slice fresh root ginger, peeled

4-6 spring onions, trimmed and sliced in half lengthways

50-75g / 2-3oz dried egg or flat rice noodles

12-14 mangetout, trimmed

1 small courgette, trimmed and sliced

6 cooked king or queen prawns, peeled

sprigs of fresh dill or coriander

1 tablespoons freshly chopped parsley

freshly ground black pepper

1. Cut the fish fillets into three or four large pieces. Place in a saucepan with the fish stock. Add the root ginger and half the spring onions. Bring to the boil and simmer for 10-15 minutes until the fish is almost cooked through.

2. Check the cooking directions on the noodles and add the noodles to the fish for the length of time given on the pack.

3. Add all the remaining ingredients and cook for a further 2-3 minutes, depending on how crunchy you like your vegetables.

4. Spoon into soup bowls and serve garnished with the remaining spring onions.

Variations

* You can use any kind of firm fish which will not flake too easily, such as plaice, cod, haddock, or monk fish.

* Try baby sweetcorn, sliced green beans or shredded lettuce leaves in place of either of the vegetables suggested above.

Rice Stick Soup
with
Pork Balls and Coriander

I have added coriander seeds and leaves to this essentially Chinese recipe and the result is quite spectacular. The flavours all marry up to make a really spicy, rich and filling soup.

175g / 6oz lean pork meat, cubed

3 spring onions, trimmed and chopped

1 large clove garlic, peeled and crushed

1 tablespoon ground coriander

1 teaspoon soy sauce

salt and freshly ground black pepper

1 tablespoon cornflour or potato flour

4 tablespoons cooking oil

600ml/1 pint chicken stock made with 1 chicken stock cube
and boiling water

1 red pepper, seeded

7cm / 3in piece cucumber

50g / 2oz rice sticks or vermicelli, broken into lengths

4-5 sprigs of fresh coriander

1. Start by making the meatballs. Place the pork, spring onion, garlic, ground coriander, soy sauce and seasoning in a food processor or blender. Process until chopped but do not run the machine for too long or the mixture will be too dense.

2. Remove the meat from the blender and shape into 10-12 small balls. Roll in cornflour or potato flour.

3. Heat the cooking oil in a frying pan or wok and fry the meatballs all over until cooked through. This will take about 4-5 minutes. Drain on kitchen paper and keep on one side.

4. Pour the stock into a saucepan and bring to the boil.

5. Cut the pepper into thin strips. Cut the piece of cucumber in half crossways and cut each half into thin sticks. Add both to the stock and simmer for 5 minutes.

6. Add the noodles and cook for 2 minutes or for the length of time given on the pack.

7. Add the pork balls and coriander a minute before the end of the cooking time.

Variations

* If you do not have a food processor or blender, look out for ready-minced pork on the supermarket shelves or ask your local butcher to mince it for you. Chop the spring onions as finely as you can.

* Use about 1cm / ½in peeled and grated fresh root ginger or 1 teaspoon grated ginger in oil in place of the coriander.

Mixed Mushroom Soup with Noodles

The more different kinds of mushrooms you can find to add to this soup the more interesting it is. If you are in a hurry you could use one of the packs of mixed sliced mushrooms on sale in some supermarkets. Simply discard any added pats of butter.

2 chicken drumsticks, skinned

6 dried mushrooms (optional)

600ml / 1 pint chicken stock made with 1 chicken stock cube and boiling water

50g / 2oz button mushrooms, sliced

50g / 2oz shitake mushrooms, sliced

50g / 2oz oyster mushrooms, thickly sliced

3 tablespoons chopped spring onions

40g / 1½oz dried egg noodles

2 tablespoons chopped coriander leaves or continental parsley

1. Place the chicken and dried mushrooms, if using, in a saucepan and cover with the stock. Bring to the boil. Cover and simmer for 20-25 minutes.

2. Remove the chicken drumsticks and take off all the meat. Return the chicken meat to the pan. Add the fresh mushrooms, spring onion and noodles.

3. Return to the boil and cook or leave to stand for the time given on the pack of noodles.

4. Spoon into soup bowls and serve garnished with fresh herbs.

Pesto Soup
with Noodles

This is a particularly quick and easy soup to make. Serve it as a substantial starter followed by a quick omelette or scrambled eggs. It is based on the Provençal pesto soup but the method has been greatly shortened.

1 tablespoon cooking oil

½ x 350g / 12oz pack frozen stir-fry vegetables

2 tablespoons pesto sauce

600ml / 1 pint stock made with 1 chicken or vegetable
stock cube and boiling water

50g / 2oz dried wholewheat or egg noodles

1. Heat the oil in a saucepan and stir-fry the vegetables for about 5 minutes or for the length of time given on the pack.

2. Stir in the pesto sauce and stock. Bring to the boil.

3. Add the noodles, return to the boil and cook or leave to stand for the length of time given on the pack.

4. Spoon into soup bowls and serve at once.

Variation
* Turn this soup into a filling main course by adding canned beans, diced cooked meats or cooked prawns.

Cantonese
Mock Bird's Nest Soup

The short lengths of rice noodles simulate the sticks and leaves of the real birds' nests in this soup from Southern China. From what I have heard of bird's nest soup, I think that even if I could afford the original I would stick with this version!

50g / 2oz bundle long rice vermicelli or rice noodles

600ml / 1 pint chicken stock made with 1½ chicken stock cubes and boiling water

4-6 mushrooms, sliced

50g / 2oz sliced ham, cut into thin strips

½ x 225g can water chestnuts, drained and sliced

4 spring onions, trimmed and chopped

1 egg white, beaten lightly

2 teaspoons freshly chopped parsley

1. Cut the rice noodles into 1cm / ½in lengths with scissors.

2. Heat the chicken stock in a large saucepan and add the mushrooms, ham, water chestnuts and spring onions. Bring to the boil and simmer for 15 minutes.

3. Add the noodles to the soup and simmer for the length of time given on the pack of noodles.

4. Stir the beaten egg white into the hot broth and serve immediately, garnishing each bowl with freshly chopped parsley.

Thai Pork Soup with Lemon Grass and Watercress

The easiest way to get a strong flavour of lemon grass into this soup is to use ready-prepared chopped lemon grass in oil. However, if you cannot find this very useful store-cupboard item, use a stick of fresh lemon grass cut into lengths with a splash of fresh lemon juice.

I tablespoon cooking oil

50g / 2oz lean pork meat, shredded

4-6 spring onions, trimmed and chopped

I teaspoon grated fresh root ginger

I teaspoon chopped lemon grass in oil

**600ml / I pint pork or chicken stock made with
I stock cube dissolved in boiling water**

½ bunch watercress

50g / 2oz beansprouts

salt and freshly ground black pepper

40g / I½oz rice vermicelli, broken up a little

sprigs of fresh parsley

1. Heat the oil in a saucepan and stir-fry the pork with the spring onions, ginger and lemon grass for 2-3 minutes.

2. Test to see that the meat is cooked through, then add all the remaining ingredients except the parsley.

3. Bring the mixture to the boil and simmer for another 2-3 minutes or for the length of time given on the pack of noodles.

4. Spoon into soup bowls and garnish with sprigs of fresh parsley. Serve at once.

Japanese Chicken Ball Soup with Seasonal Greens

This soup makes a great starter when you are entertaining as it looks really colourful and tastes superb. Just double up the quantities for 4 people.

1 boned chicken breast fillet, skinned

4 spring onions, trimmed and cut into short lengths

½ small egg

1 teaspoon cornflour

2 teaspoons soy sauce

salt and freshly ground black pepper

600ml / 1 pint chicken stock made with 1 chicken stock cube and boiling water

1 tablespoon sherry

a few slivers of fresh root ginger

sprigs of fresh coriander

40g / 1½oz Chinese leaves, bok choy, spinach or any seasonal greens, coarsely shredded

50g / 2oz dried egg or wheat noodles

1. Start by making the chicken balls. Cut the chicken meat into pieces and mix with a quarter of the spring onions. Mince the mixture finely or process in a food processor.

2. Mix with the egg, half the cornflour, 1 teaspoon soy sauce and seasoning. Shape into small balls about the size of a walnut. Roll in the remaining cornflour.

3. Heat the chicken stock in a saucepan with the remaining soy sauce, the sherry, root ginger and coriander. Bring to the boil and reduce the heat to medium.

4. Carefully add the chicken balls, one at a time, making sure that they are not touching each other. Simmer for 4 minutes.

5. Add the shredded Chinese leaves to the broth and cook for a further 2 minutes. Check that the chicken balls have cooked through.

6. Plunge the noodles into boiling water and cook or leave to stand for the length of time given on the pack.

7. Drain the noodles well and spoon into soup bowls. Top with the chicken balls and their stock and garnish with the remaining spring onion.

Miso Soup
with Tofu and
Cellophane Noodles

I like this soup made with bean or rice noodles, but there is no reason why you should not use the more traditional Japanese or Chinese noodles.

600ml / 1 pint vegetable stock made with 1 vegetable stock cube and boiling water

6 spring onions, trimmed and cut into short lengths

1cm / ½in piece fresh root ginger, peeled and cut into thin sticks

50g / 2oz green beans or mangetout, trimmed and cut into lengths

75g / 3oz cellophane or rice noodles

1 tablespoon miso paste

125g / 4oz tofu, cut into small cubes

sprigs of continental or broadleaf parsley

1. Pour the stock into a saucepan and bring to the boil.

2. Add the spring onions, ginger and beans or mangetout. Return to the boil and cook for 5 minutes.

3. Next add the noodles and continue to cook over a medium heat for the length of time given on the pack of noodles.

4. Remove the pan from the heat and stir in the miso paste. The soup should not be boiled again after this has been added.

5. Spoon into soup bowls and top with tofu and parsley. Serve at once.

Variation
* Tofu has a good texture for this soup but if you cannot find it or do not like it, you could use half the quantity of Halloumi cheese.

Tuscan
Bean and Noodle Soup
with Garlic

The flavour of this Italian speciality improves slightly with standing and reheating, but don't leave it for too long or the pasta will soak up all the liquid! Complete the meal with grilled Italian sausages or poussin roast with olive oil and sage.

2 tablespoons olive oil

2 large cloves garlic, peeled and thinly sliced

1 x 225g / 8oz can chopped tomatoes

450ml / ¾ pint chicken or vegetable stock made with stock cube and boiling water

4 tablespoons canned and drained cannellini beans

1 tablespoon freshly chopped basil

50g / 2oz fresh Italian noodles cut into 5cm / 2in lengths

2 large sprigs of fresh basil leaves

1. Heat the oil in a saucepan and fry the sliced garlic until lightly browned.

2. Remove from the heat and stir in the tomatoes. (If you put them in over the heat the oil may splash you). Return to the heat and bring to the boil.

3. Next add the stock and all the remaining ingredients except for the sprigs of fresh basil leaves. Simmer for 5 minutes.

4. Spoon into soup bowls and garnish with the basil sprigs.

Variation
* Add diced bacon bits and fry with the garlic.

Thai
Coconut Milk Soup
with Prawns and Egg Noodles

This is one of my favourite soups and despite the fact that it is made in a European kitchen, it has a real Thai flavour to it. It is best made with large cooked and shelled king prawns but these can be expensive. Smaller cocktail prawns or Pacific prawns may not look so attractive but they taste almost as good and are a lot easier on the pocket.

To enhance the authenticity of the soup serve it exactly as it is but do warn your partner or guest about the sliced ginger, which they may find too strongly flavoured to crunch, and the stick of lemon grass and bayleaves, which of course should not be eaten.

2 tablespoons dried coconut milk

450ml / ¾ pint water

½ chicken stock cube

I teaspoon lemon grass in oil or I large stick fresh lemon grass

10 fresh coriander leaves, retaining 4 for garnish

2 bayleaves

I small onion or 2-3 shallots, peeled and thinly sliced

2.5cm / Iin piece fresh root ginger, peeled and thinly sliced

I clove garlic, peeled and thinly sliced

40g / I½oz dried egg noodles, broken slightly

125g / 4oz cooked king prawns or small cooked prawns

1. Mix 150ml / ¼ pint of the water with the coconut milk. Take care not to allow it to form into lumps.

2. Bring the rest of the water to the boil in a saucepan and dissolve the stock cube in it. Add the coconut milk, lemon grass, coriander and bayleaves and return to the boil.

3. Add the onion or shallots, root ginger and garlic. Reduce the heat and simmer over a low heat for 10 minutes.

4. Add the noodles and prawns and boil for a further minute. Cook or leave to stand for the time given on the pack of noodles.

5. Pour into soup bowls and serve immediately, garnished with the reserved fresh coriander leaves.

Variation
* Add fresh vegetables with the prawns such as mangetout, baby sweetcorn or shredded greens.

DOUBLE QUICK
NOODLES

The recipes in this chapter only take about 10-15 minutes to prepare, and some of them can be produced even more quickly. They are ideal for anyone who has to dash back from work, eat a quick meal and go out again. Served with a tossed green salad and fruit to follow, any of these dishes will provide an extremely healthy and nutritious meal.

Very quick noodle meals are made by tossing fresh or quick-cook noodles in oil, cream or soft cheese with a lot of freshly chopped herbs. Most supermarkets now have a great array of fresh herbs during the spring, summer and autumn months and you can usually get fresh parsley all the year round. There are also boxes of frozen herbs which you can sprinkle straight from the freezer, as well as herbs packed in oil.

Alternatively, you can give an oriental feel to your meal with garlic, fresh root ginger and lemon grass, all available fresh or chopped, grated and packed in oil. Sesame oil, toasted sesame seeds and soy sauce complete the effect. Other very quick ideas include tossing noodles in olive, sun-dried tomato, pepper or artichoke paste, tapenade or pesto sauce.

Fresh Noodles with Walnut and Blue Cheese Sauce

Tossing fresh noodles in cream and cheese must be one of the quickest ways of preparing noodles. It is also one of the most versatile dishes as you can use almost any kind of well flavoured soft cheese and a variety of nuts. For ideas see below. If you are worried about the fat content of this dish you can substitute low fat fromage frais for cream - but do not allow the mixture to boil. Yoghurt is another alternative but this will need to be stabilised with a little cornflour.

225-300g / 8-10oz fresh tagliatelle or flat noodles

salt

1 tablespoon olive oil

150ml / ¼ pint single cream

75-125g / 3-4oz Dolcelatte Italian blue cheese, cut into small pieces

50g / 2oz walnuts, chopped

freshly ground black pepper

1. Put the fresh noodles into a large saucepan with plenty of salted boiling water and a little olive oil. Continue to boil for 2-3 minutes until just tender to the bite. Drain very well and keep warm.

2. Pour the cream into the empty pan and stir in the cheese. Allow to melt and bring to the boil. Return the pasta to the pan and toss in the cream and cheese mixture with most of the walnuts.

3. Transfer to a serving dish and sprinkle with the remaining nuts and pepper. Serve at once.

Variations

* Dolcelatte is a fairly mild blue cheese; you will produce stronger flavours with Stilton, Gorgonzola or Roquefort.

* Fresh or soft goat's cheeses are also very good and are not as strongly flavoured as you might think. Try toasted pinenuts or almonds with these.

* Camembert and Brie also work well with chopped hazelnuts or roasted peanuts.

Ham and Eggs
with Buckwheat Noodles

Ham and Eggs is a universal dish which is welcome at any time of the day. This version is derived from Italian Carbonara which is said to have been the Italian cooks' answer to the GI's demand for 'Ham 'n Eggs' during the liberation of Italy. For an even faster to prepare dish, choose Japanese buckwheat ramen or fresh Italian noodles which will both cook in 2-3 minutes.

125g / 4oz buckwheat noodles

salt

15g / ½oz butter

50g / 2oz cooked ham, chopped

3 eggs (size 3), beaten

freshly ground black pepper

1. Plunge the buckwheat noodles into a large saucepan of boiling salted water and cook for the length of time given on the pack.

2. Drain the noodles, return to the pan and toss in the butter. Add the ham and return the pan to the heat.

3. Season the eggs with black pepper, stir well and pour over the noodles. Toss the noodles in the eggs over a medium heat. When the eggs start to curdle and coat the noodles, remove the pan from the heat. The eggs will finish cooking in the heat from the noodles. They should not be too well cooked.

4. Spoon onto warm plates and serve with more black pepper.

Variations

* Stir 25g / 1oz freshly grated Parmesan cheese into the beaten eggs before adding to the noodles.

* Stir 2 tablespoons freshly chopped parsley, chervil or tarragon into the beaten eggs.

Fresh Noodles with Tomatoes, Cheese and Olives

This mouth-watering mound of noodles and stringy cheese can be rustled up very quickly indeed. It is particularly good served with a salad of piquant leaves such as rocket, chicory, watercress or curly endives.

I tablespoon olive or cooking oil

I small onion, peeled and finely chopped

I x 225g / 8oz can tomatoes

I tablespoon tomato purée

¼ teaspoon dried oregano

pinch dried mixed herbs

salt and freshly ground black pepper

225-300g / 8-10oz fresh Italian noodles

I teaspoon olive or cooking oil

25g / 1oz butter

200g / 7oz Mozzarella cheese, cubed

50g / 2oz Parmesan cheese, grated

50g / 2oz stoned black olives, sliced

1. Heat the olive oil in a saucepan and fry the onion gently for 2-3 minutes. Add the contents of the can of tomatoes, the tomato purée, herbs and seasoning. Break up the tomatoes with a wooden spoon and bring the sauce to the boil. Reduce the heat to medium and cook for 10 minutes.

2. Place the noodles in a large saucepan with plenty of salted boiling water and a little olive oil. Cook for about 2-3 minutes until the pasta is just tender to the bite. Drain well.

3. Place the noodles in a large heated serving bowl and add the butter, Mozzarella cheese and half the Parmesan. Toss thoroughly and then top with the tomato sauce, the sliced olives and the remaining Parmesan.

4. Sprinkle with more freshly ground black pepper and serve.

Quick Tossed Vegetable Noodles

Your choice of stir-fry sauce will give the definitive flavour to this really quick noodle dish. I have tried it with yellow bean sauce, sweet chilli sauce and Chinese oyster sauce.

½ x 250g / 9oz pack dried egg or wheat noodles

2 tablespoons cooking oil

1 x 300g / 10oz pack frozen stir-fry vegetables

1 teaspoon lemon grass in oil or 2 sticks lemon grass cut into pieces

3-4 tablespoons stir-fry sauce

1. Plunge the noodles into a large saucepan of boiling water and cook or leave to stand for the time given on the pack.

2. Heat the cooking oil in a wok or deep frying pan and stir-fry the frozen vegetable mix for the length of time given on the pack.

3. Stir in the lemon grass and stir-fry sauce and mix well. Bring to the boil.

4. Drain the noodles well and add to the pan with the vegetables. Toss well together and serve at once.

Variation

* Use crushed garlic in place of lemon grass and add a pinch of five spice powder if you have it.

* Add diced cooked ham, cold meats or cooked chicken to taste.

* Use fresh green vegetables in place of frozen vegetables, such as finely shredded courgettes, green pepper, celery sticks and spinach. Garnish with celery leaves.

Fresh Noodles
with Boursin and Peas

Soft cheese makes a really quick sauce base for noodles. Fromage frais, curd cheese, German quark, cottage cheese, and Philadelphia cream cheese all work well. However, flavoured cheeses such as Boursin and garlic or herb roulade save you having to add very much in the way of other seasonings.

125g / 4oz herb-flavoured soft cheese, such as Boursin

2 tablespoons cream

225-300g / 8-10oz fresh noodles

salt

75g / 3oz cooked peas

freshly ground black pepper

2 tablespoons freshly chopped chervil, parsley or mint

1. Heat the cheese in a small saucepan with the cream and stir until all the cheese has melted.

2. Plunge the noodles into a large saucepan of salted boiling water, taking care not to allow the water to leave the boil. Cook for 2-3 minutes until the noodles are just tender. Drain the noodles well.

3. Return the cheese mixture to the heat and add the peas, black pepper and herbs. Bring to the boil and pour over the noodles. Toss well and serve at once.

Fresh Noodles
Tossed with Baked Beans
and Cheddar Cheese

The idea of this unlikely combination came from a friend of mine who works from home and needs to grab a nourishing but quick meal between sessions on the word processor and work in the garden! I tried it out and added not a thing - it is very good indeed.

1 x 425g / 14oz can baked bean

1 tablespoon tomato purée (optional)

225-300g / 8-10oz fresh noodles

salt

125g / 4oz mature Cheddar cheese, grated

freshly ground black pepper

3 tablespoons freshly chopped basil leaves

1. Empty the contents of the can of baked beans into a small saucepan and stir in the tomato purée if using. Gently heat through over a low heat.

2. Plunge the noodles into a large saucepan of boiling salted water and return to the boil. Cook for 2-3 minutes until the noodles are just tender.

3. Drain the noodles. Add the hot baked beans and toss well together. Add half the cheese and the pepper and toss again.

4. Spoon into individual dishes and top with the remaining cheese and chopped basil. Serve at once.

Variations

* Use curried baked beans or add a little curry paste or garam masala when heating the beans.

* Substitute fresh coriander for basil and serve with chutney on the side.

Noodles
with
Sweetcorn and Herbs

This is the recipe to use when you are really in a hurry. It can be made in just 8 minutes if you use a proprietary brand of Chinese dried egg noodles which reconstitute in 5 minutes, less if you use quick noodles.

½ x 250g / 9oz pack dried egg or wheat noodles

1 x 200g / 7oz can whole sweetcorn kernels or Mexicorn, drained

2 tablespoons mayonnaise

3-4 tablespoons freshly chopped chervil or parsley

plenty of freshly ground black pepper

2 tablespoons dry roasted peanuts or toasted pinenuts

salt to taste

1. Plunge the noodles into a saucepan of boiling water and cook or leave to stand for the time given on the pack.

2. Drain and toss over a low heat with all the remaining ingredients. Serve at once.

Variations
* To make a more substantial dish, stir in 125g / 4oz cottage cheese just before serving. Toss over a low heat and serve at once.

* Mayonnaise makes a good creamy base for noodle dishes. Choose plain, lemon or garlic versions, to taste.

Cardamom Eggs
with Courgettes
and Chinese Noodles

This is a real East meets West recipe. It is based on egg and courgette dishes from Italy and cardamom and vegetable combinations from the Orient. The result is extremely good.

225g / 8oz courgettes, trimmed

½ x 250g / 9oz pack dried egg or wheat noodles

25g / 1oz butter or a mixture of butter and cooking oil

seeds from 2-3 cardamom pods

2 shallots or ½ small onion, peeled and finely chopped

3 large eggs, beaten

2 tablespoons water

freshly ground black pepper

1. Cut the courgettes into thin sticks about 2.5cm / 1in in length.

2. Plunge the noodles into a saucepan of boiling water. Cook or leave to stand for the length of time given on the pack.

3. Heat the butter with the cardamom seeds in a non-stick wok or deep frying pan. Add the shallots and courgette sticks and stir-fry for a couple of minutes until the vegetables are just beginning to soften.

4. Beat the eggs and water together and pour over the vegetables. Stir-fry the eggs so that they do not set into a solid mass but not so vigorously as to scramble them.

5. Drain the noodles well and add to the pan just before the eggs set completely. Toss with black pepper and serve.

Variation
* Use 2 tablespoons freshly chopped dill in place of the cardamom seeds.

Scottish Salmon and Cream Sauce for Fresh Noodles

Most supermarkets and delicatessen shops sell off-cuts of smoked salmon which are much cheaper than sliced smoked salmon. These can be used to very good effect in this quick dish.

75g / 3oz smoked salmon off-cuts

150ml / ¼ pint double cream

25g / 1oz butter

salt and freshly ground black pepper

225-300g / 8-10oz fresh noodles

1 tablespoon freshly chopped dill

1. Remove any bones or very dark brown pieces from the smoked salmon and chop finely.

2. Put the cream, butter and seasonings into a large saucepan and bring to the boil. Simmer fast for 3-4 minutes to thicken the cream. Stir from time to time.

3. Plunge the noodles into lightly salted boiling water and cook for 2-3 minutes until just tender. Drain well.

4. Add the chopped smoked salmon and the dill to the pan of cream. Stir and add the noodles. Toss and serve at once.

Variation
* Add a teaspoonful of mild grainy mustard with the cream.

Egg Noodles
with
Indonesian Sauce

It is worth looking out for creamed coconut, for it not only gives a wonderful flavour to the sauce but also gives it a very smooth and velvety texture.

½ x 250g / 9oz pack dried egg noodles

I tablespoon cooking oil

5mm / ¼ in piece fresh root ginger, cut into thin strips

2 onions, peeled and sliced

50g / 2oz French beans, trimmed

175g / 6oz Chinese leaves, sliced

50g / 2oz beansprouts

2 tablespoons dry roasted or toasted peanuts

2 teaspoons soy sauce

Sauce:

2 tablespoons peanut butter

100ml / 4fl oz hot water

15g / ½oz creamed coconut (optional)

I tablespoon soy sauce

½ clove garlic, peeled and crushed

1-2 tablespoons lemon juice

1. To make the sauce, mix the peanut butter with the hot water. Stir in all the remaining ingredients and bring to the boil, stirring all the time. Remove from the heat and keep warm.

2. Plunge the dried egg noodles in a pan of boiling water and cook or leave to stand for the time given on the pack.

3. Heat the cooking oil in a wok or deep frying pan and quickly stir-fry

the root ginger and onions. Add the French beans and continue to stir-fry for 2-3 minutes. Add the Chinese leaves, beansprouts and nuts. Toss over the heat for a further 2-3 minutes. The vegetables should soften but remain crisp in the centre.

4. Drain the noodles well and toss with the vegetables. Sprinkle on the soy sauce.

5. Serve on individual plates with the Indonesian sauce spooned over the top.

Variation
* Substitute 1 teaspoon of molasses or black treacle for the creamed coconut.

Buckwheat Noodles
with
Quick Prawn Sauce

The inspiration for this recipe is very definitely Japanese and I usually use those small packets of buckwheat ramen which come with their own little packets of dried stock powder. This gives a very authentic flavour.

The dish has a fairly runny sauce, so start the meal with something firmer such as fried tofu with freshly grated ginger or grilled vegetables with a splash of roasted sesame oil.

2 x 90g / 3½oz pack Japanese buckwheat ramen or noodles with dried stock

4-6 spring onions

I tablespoon cooking oil

75g / 3oz mangetout, trimmed and stringed if necessary

200g / 7oz cooked and peeled king prawns

I tablespoon rice vinegar

I tablespoon tamari sauce

4-5 tablespoons water

1. Fill a saucepan with water and bring to the boil. Add the buckwheat ramen, keeping the dried stock on one side. Return the water to the boil and simmer the ramen for 5 minutes or for the length of time given on the pack.

2. Cut the spring onions into short lengths, cutting diagonally across the stems. Use both the white and the green part of the onion.

3. Heat the cooking oil in a small deep frying pan and stir-fry the onions for about a minute. Add the mangetout and continue to stir-fry for another minute or so.

4. Add all the remaining ingredients and bring to the boil. Sprinkle one of the packets of dried stock from the ramen over the top and stir well. Continue to simmer for another minute, stirring all the time.

5. Drain the ramen and pile into a serving dish. Spoon the prawn mixture over the top and serve at once.

Variation

* If you do not have Japanese rice vinegar or tamari sauce to hand you can change the flavour of the dish to Chinese by using ordinary vinegar and 2 tablespoons soy sauce with a dash of five spice powder. If you do this you will not need the dried stock mixture, so keep it on one side to make soup later. Alternatively, use dried egg noodles instead.

Delaware Chicken Livers
with
Fresh Noodles and Sage

You can use virtually any kind of noodles for this unusual American dish with chicken livers. Fresh noodles would probably be the American choice, and they are also the quickest to cook.

225g / 8oz fresh noodles

salt and freshly ground black pepper

25g / 1oz butter

1 teaspoon cooking oil

125g / 4oz chicken livers, washed, dried and cut in half

¼ teaspoon dried sage (or 1 teaspoon frozen), well-crushed

50g / 2oz ham, finely chopped

2 tablespoons dry or medium sherry

1. Plunge the noodles into a saucepan of salted boiling water and cook for about 2-3 minutes until just tender. Drain very well and toss in half the butter.

2. Heat the rest of the butter and oil in a frying pan and fry the chicken livers gently on all sides.

3. Add the seasoning and sage and continue to fry for about 2-3 minutes until the livers are cooked through. Take care not to over-cook the livers or they will go hard. Add the ham and toss with the cooked livers.

4. Spoon the noodles onto individual plates and top with the liver and ham.

5. Pour the sherry into the pan in which the livers were cooked and quickly bring to the boil, stirring all the time. Pour the liquid over the livers and noodles and serve at once.

THIRTY MINUTE
NOODLE DISHES

Recipes in this section take up to about 30 minutes to prepare *and* cook. They use dried egg, wholewheat, wheat, buckwheat and rice noodles as well as fresh noodles and a whole host of other ingredients which are easy to find in most shops.

Stir-frying is a very quick method of cooking and I have used this technique in quite a few of the recipes. In an ideal world this should be done in a wok, but a deep-sided frying pan works pretty well too – you just have to be more careful not to knock the food out of the frying pan as you toss it around in the pan. I find that it is easier to use a non-stick wok or frying pan for stir-frying, but this is not essential.

What is essential is to heat the cooking oil to a high temperature before you start to cook. This ensures that the food is sealed as it hits the fat. Keep the temperature fairly high while you are stir-frying and keep the food on the move. If you leave it to stand it will take up fat and may burn on one side and remain uncooked on the other.

Cut all the pieces of food to be stir-fried to about the same size. This helps the food to cook evenly and ensures that each piece of chicken, broccoli or whatever is ready at the same time.

Stir-fried vegetables are very good if they are still rather crunchy but if you prefer them not too hard, cover the pan with a lid after adding liquid ingredients such as stock, soy sauce or rice vinegar and steam for 2-3 minutes.

Unlike vegetables, meat must be fully cooked so check that strips of pork or chicken are cooked through – when you cut a sample piece in half, there should be no sign of pinkness in the centre. If there is, stir-fry for a little longer.

Neapolitan Sauce
for Fresh Noodles

The punchy flavours of this quickly made sauce are typical of Southern Italy. The sauce is just as good served in the dead of winter as in the heat of the summer. Start the meal with a warming soup or light salad, depending on the time of the year, and finish with Tiramasu.

1 tablespoon olive oil

1 onion, peeled and finely chopped

125g / 4oz French beans, trimmed and cut into lengths

2 tomatoes, coarsely chopped

50g / 2oz salami, cut in one thick slice, diced

50g / 2oz ham sausage, cut in one thick slice, diced

6-8 black olives, stoned and cut into quarters

225-300g / 8-10oz fresh noodles

freshly ground black pepper

freshly grated Parmesan cheese

1. Heat the olive oil in a wok or deep frying pan and stir-fry the onion and beans for 2-3 minutes. Add the tomatoes and cook for a further 2-3 minutes.

2. Next add the salami, ham sausage and olives and toss over a medium heat.

3. Plunge the noodles into a large saucepan of boiling water and cook for 2-3 minutes until just tender.

4. Drain well and add to the salami mixture. Season with black pepper and toss well together. Serve with a bowl of grated Parmesan cheese on the side.

Variation
* Use Italian mortadella in place of both the salami and ham sausage.

Pork and Pepper Stir-fry
with Chinese Noodles

This colourful and very quickly prepared dish can be made with any of the good proprietary stir-fry sauces on the market. I used a Chinese barbecue sauce when I was testing, but you could use black or yellow bean sauce or Hoisin sauce.

¼ x 250g / 9oz pack dried egg noodles

salt and freshly ground pepper

2 tablespoons cooking oil

I clove garlic, peeled and chopped

Icm / ½in piece fresh root ginger, peeled and grated

225g / 8oz lean pork, cut into long thin strips across the grain

½ onion, peeled and sliced

½ green pepper, seeded and thinly sliced

½ red pepper, seeded and thinly sliced

½ yellow pepper, seeded and thinly sliced

50ml / 2fl oz Chinese barbecue stir-fry sauce

I teaspoon soy sauce

1. Plunge the noodles into a pan of boiling salted water. Cook or leave to stand for the length of time given on the pack.

2. Heat 1 tablespoon of cooking oil in a non-stick wok or frying pan and fry the garlic and ginger for half a minute.

3. Add the pork and stir-fry for 2-3 minutes until all trace of pinkness has left the meat. Cut one piece in half to be sure the meat is cooked through. Remove the meat from the pan and keep warm.

4. Add the remaining oil to the pan, heat through and add the onion and peppers. Stir-fry for 2-3 minutes to soften. Add the pork and pour on the stir-fry sauce, soy sauce and seasoning. Bring the mixture to the boil and cook fast for 2-3 minutes.

5. Drain the noodles well and toss with the pork and pepper mixture.

Tarragon Chicken
with Carrots and Noodles

Tarragon is delicious with carrots. In France, it is also a traditional accompaniment to chicken in cream sauce. As I am particularly fond of tarragon, I decided to put the two ideas together and here is the result. I hope you like it as much as I do.

2 medium-sized carrots, peeled

15g / ½oz butter

2 teaspoons cooking oil

2 shallots or ½ small onion, peeled and thinly sliced

2 chicken breast fillets or 4 thighs, skinned and boned

100ml / 4fl oz double cream

50ml / 2fl oz chicken stock

2 tablespoons freshly chopped tarragon

salt and freshly ground black pepper

½ x 250g / 9oz pack dried egg or wheat noodles

1. Slice the carrots as thinly as you can and steam in a steamer or a very little water for 10 minutes.

2. Heat the butter and oil in a wok or deep frying pan and fry the shallots or onion for a minute or so. Add the chicken pieces and stir-fry for 3-4 minutes.

3. Check that the chicken is cooked through by cutting a piece in half. There should be no sign of pinkness.

4. Add the cooked carrots, cream, stock, tarragon and seasoning and bring to the boil. Cook over a medium heat for 2-3 minutes to reduce the sauce a little. Stir from time to time.

5. Plunge the noodles into boiling water and cook or leave to stand for the length of time given on the pack. Drain noodles well.

6. Place noodles on individual plates and spoon the tarragon chicken and carrots over the top.

McKenzie Noodles

This idea comes from a vegetarian friend who often experiments with different combinations of vegetables. Potatoes may seem an odd ingredient for a noodle dish but in some parts of Northern Italy it is standard fare. Try it and see what you think.

12-16 new potatoes, depending on size

8-12 baby sweetcorn

125g / 4oz broccoli florets

225g / 8oz fresh noodles

1 tablespoon mayonnaise

3 tablespoons freshly chopped chives

salt and freshly ground black pepper

1. Steam the new potatoes and sweetcorn in a steamer or in very little boiling water until just cooked. This will take about 8-10 minutes depending on the size of the vegetables.

2. Add the broccoli florets about 3-4 minutes before the end of the cooking time.

3. Plunge the noodles into a large saucepan of boiling water and cook for 2-3 minutes until just tender. Drain well.

4. Toss the noodles in the mayonnaise and add the vegetables, chives and seasoning. Toss again and serve.

Variations

* Use freshly chopped mint or chervil in place of chives or a mixture of two of them.

* Use diced courgettes in place of broccoli florets.

Gammon and Courgette Stir-fry with Rice Sticks

This is a particularly colourful dish which I often serve when I have friends for supper. The quantities double up perfectly. Start the meal with a Hummous or Taramasalata dip and pitta bread and finish with a fresh pineapple or peaches.

125-175g / 4-6oz rice sticks or flat rice noodles

I tablespoon cooking oil

2.5cm / I in piece fresh root ginger, peeled and grated

½ bunch spring onions, trimmed and sliced

2 small gammon steaks (about 225-300g / 8-10oz in total), cut into thin strips

175g / 6oz courgettes, sliced

50g / 2oz baby sweetcorn

2-3 sticks celery, finely sliced

I tablespoon soy sauce

I tablespoon sherry

freshly ground black pepper

1. Plunge the rice noodles into a saucepan of boiling water and cook for the length of time given on the pack.

2. Heat half the cooking oil in a deep frying pan or wok and stir-fry the ginger and spring onions for 1 minute. Add the gammon strips and stir-fry for 3 minutes until cooked through. Transfer to a plate and keep warm.

3. Add the remaining cooking oil to the pan and stir-fry the vegetables for 2 minutes. Return the gammon to the pan and add the soy sauce and sherry and boil fast for a minute. Season with black pepper.

4. Drain the noodles very well and add to the pan of gammon and courgettes. Toss well together and serve.

Wholewheat Noodles with Beans

This Hungarian inspired recipe should be served with large flat noodles which are popular in Eastern Europe. However, it is also very good with any kind of wholewheat noodles. Serve with a salad of lettuce mixed with piquant leaves such as watercress, rocket or sorrel.

½ x 250g / 9oz pack wholewheat noodles or 2 x 90g / 3½oz packs Japanese wholewheat ramen

I tablespoon cooking oil

I onion, peeled and chopped

I clove garlic, peeled and crushed (optional)

I x 225g / 8oz can tomatoes

I x 225g / 8oz can baked beans

I teaspoon sugar

I tablespoon hot paprika pepper

freshly ground black pepper

2 small dill pickled cucumbers, diced

2-4 sprigs fresh dill

1. Plunge the noodles into a large saucepan of boiling water and cook for the length of time given on the pack.

2. Heat the cooking oil in a saucepan and gently fry the onion and garlic, if using, for 2-3 minutes.

3. Empty the contents of the two cans into the pan and add the sugar, paprika and black pepper. Bring the mixture to the boil and simmer for 5 minutes. Stir in the cucumber.

4. Drain the noodles and pile onto serving plates. Top with the sauce and garnish with fresh dill.

Variations

* Add diced smoked bacon to the pan with the garlic and onions.

* For a really rich dish add 2-3 tablespoons soured cream.

Pepper Noodles
with Ham

This method of cooking peppers may seem a bit fiddly but it gives them a wonderful barbecued flavour. It also makes them much easier to peel.

I red pepper, seeded and quartered

I green pepper, seeded and quartered

½ x 250g / 9oz pack dried wheat noodles

2 tablespoons olive oil

125g / 4oz thick-cut cooked ham, cut into strips

50g / 2oz black olives, stoned

a little fresh or dried wild marjoram or oregano

2 heaped teaspoons mayonnaise

1. Place the peppers under the grill, skin side up and cook until well seared. Leave to cool a little, then peel and cut into strips.

2. Plunge the noodles into boiling water and cook or leave to stand for the time given on the pack. Drain well.

3. Heat the oil in a deep saucepan and add the noodles. Toss well and add the pepper strips, cooked ham, olives and herbs. Toss again over a low heat to thoroughly warm through.

4. Spoon onto individual plates and top with a spoonful of mayonnaise.

Variations

* Use garlic- or lemon-flavoured mayonnaise to add variety.

* Use oregano or basil in place of marjoram.

Chinese-style Stir-fried Vegetables with Halloumi Cheese

Make up your own mix of vegetables for this fast stir-fry using whatever you have to hand in the vegetable bin or salad drawer. Don't be afraid to include radishes, cucumber or watercress as well as carrots, cabbage, beans, sweetcorn, sugar peas or beansprouts.

Halloumi cheese is unusual in that it does not melt in the heat but remains intact. However, if you cook it for too long it will seize up and become rather unpleasant.

½ x 250g / 9oz pack dried egg noodles

2 tablespoons cooking oil

I clove garlic, peeled and crushed

½ bunch spring onions, trimmed and coarsely chopped

Icm / ½in piece fresh root ginger, peeled and grated

I small red pepper, seeded and finely shredded

125g / 4oz mixed vegetables to hand

2-3 tablespoons sherry

3 tablespoons vegetable stock

pinch five spice powder

salt and freshly ground black pepper

125g / 4oz Halloumi cheese, finely diced

1. Plunge the noodles into boiling water and cook for the time given on the pack.

2. Heat the oil in a wok or deep frying pan and stir-fry the garlic, spring onions and ginger for 1 minute.

3. Add the pepper and continue stir-frying for another 2 minutes. Next add the vegetables and toss the contents of the pan well together.

4. Add the liquid ingredients, five spice powder and seasonings and turn up the heat. Cook for another 1-2 minutes, stirring all the time.

5. Drain the noodles and add to the vegetables with the cheese. Toss over a high heat for about half a minute. Serve at once.

Variations

* Add a few drops of sesame oil to the cooking oil and sprinkle the finished dish with toasted sesame seeds.

* Use Feta cheese in place of Halloumi cheese. This will give a more piquant flavour and a creamier texture.

Buckwheat Noodles
with Chilli Beef

This recipe makes quite a hot chilli beef, but you can tone it down by cutting down on the fresh green chilli. Serve with a salad of mixed grated carrots and cucumber tossed in yogurt.

I tablespoon cooking oil

I small onion, peeled and finely chopped

I clove garlic, peeled and crushed (optional)

I fresh green chilli pepper, seeded and finely chopped

225g / 8oz lean minced beef

I teaspoon ground cumin

I tablespoon plain flour

pinch mixed dried herbs

salt

Tabasco sauce

125g / 4oz buckwheat noodles

1. Heat the cooking oil in a saucepan and add the onion, garlic if using, and the green chilli. Gently fry for 2-3 minutes.

2. Stir in the beef and turn up the heat to brown all over. Reduce the heat and add all the remaining ingredients except the Tabasco sauce and noodles. Bring to the boil and simmer for 15-20 minutes.

3. Gradually plunge the buckwheat noodles into a large saucepan of boiling water, taking care not to allow the water to go off the boil. Cook for the length of time given on the pack. Drain well.

4. Taste the beef mixture and add Tabasco sauce if you would prefer it hotter.

5. Spoon the noodles onto individual plates and top with the chilli beef.

Variation

* Substitute a small can of red kidney beans for half the beef and add an extra fresh chilli, or dried ground chilli.

Chicken Cacciatore with Flat Noodles

There are as many different recipes for this colourful mixture of tomatoes and chicken as there are Italian cooks, but they are nearly always served with some kind of noodles, ranging from tagliatelle to lasangnette.

2 chicken leg joints or 3-4 thighs

2 tablespoons olive oil

I onion, peeled and sliced

50g / 2oz mushrooms, sliced

½ teaspoon fresh or ¼ teaspoon dried rosemary

pinch of dried thyme

salt and freshly ground black pepper

2-3 tablespoons cider or wine vinegar

225g / 8oz can tomatoes

I tablespoon tomato purée

8-10 black olives

175g / 6oz dried flat Italian noodles

1. If you are using chicken joints cut them across the joint into thighs and drumsticks. Remove the skin from all the pieces and cut the thigh pieces into two again.

2. Heat the oil in a deep pan. Add the chicken, onion, mushrooms and herbs and toss over a medium heat until the chicken has sealed and everything has taken on a good colour. This takes about 4-5 minutes.

3. Add the seasoning and pour on the vinegar, the contents of the can of tomatoes and the tomato purée. Break up the tomatoes with a fork. Bring the mixture to the boil and cook over a medium heat, stirring from time to time.

4. Add the olives after 15 minutes and continue to cook for a further 5-10 minutes until the chicken is cooked through.

5. Meanwhile cook the dried noodles in lightly salted boiling water for about 8-9 minutes or for the length of time given on the pack. Drain and toss with a little olive oil,then serve with the chicken.

American Shrimps with Cellophane Noodles

Often known as Shrimp Long Rice in California, this typical East meets West dish is very runny. I used Chinese rice noodles called "Sha Ho Fun" which are rather like tagliatelle.

200g / 7oz cooked king prawns or large warm water shrimps

1 tablespoon soy sauce

½ teaspoon grated fresh root ginger

2 cloves garlic, peeled and minced

1 teaspoon sugar

salt and freshly ground black pepper

½ x 250g / 9oz bundle long rice sticks or cellophane noodles

2 tablespoons cooking oil

50g / 2oz baby sweetcorn, cut in half lengthways

2 large sticks celery, finely sliced

6 spring onions, trimmed and cut into 5cm / 2in lengths on the slant

300ml / ½ pint chicken stock made with 1 chicken stock cube and boiling water

1 tablespoon freshly chopped chives

1. Place the prawns in a bowl. Mix together the soy sauce, root ginger, garlic, sugar and seasoning, then pour over the prawns. Leave to stand for 20 minutes, turning from time to time.

2. Meanwhile, plunge the noodles into a saucepan of boiling water and cook for the length of time given on the pack.

3. Heat the oil in a deep saucepan and stir-fry the vegetables for 2 minutes.

4. Drain the noodles very well and add to the pan of vegetables with the prawn mixture and the stock. Bring to the boil and simmer for 5 minutes.

5. Spoon into bowls and sprinkle with chives. Serve at once.

Variation

* Use a thinly sliced, uncooked chicken breast in place of the prawns. This will take a little longer to cook through in the broth. Allow about 10-15 minutes and add the noodles 5 minutes before the end of the cooking time.

* Use mangetout or sugar peas in place of sweetcorn and use mint instead of chives.

Teryaki Plaice
with Egg Noodles

You can, if you prefer, roll up the plaice fillets and cook them in a steamer rather than flat on the plate. Use half quantities of soy sauce and stock and steam for 8-10 minutes, depending on the thickness of the plaice fillets.

½ x 250g / 9oz pack dried egg noodles

a little cooking oil

1 teaspoon grated fresh root ginger

6-8 spring onions, trimmed and finely chopped

freshly ground black pepper

2 large fillets of plaice

1 tablespoon soy or tamari sauce

1 tablespoon fish stock or water

1. Plunge the noodles into boiling water and cook or leave to stand for the time given on the pack.

2. Brush two large dinner plates with a very little oil and place each one on top of a pan of water. Bring to the boil.

3. Mix the ginger with the spring onions, season with pepper and spread over the fish. Transfer to the plates.

4. Mix together the soy sauce and stock or water and pour half over each fish. Cover with two smaller plates and cook for 5-7 minutes, depending on the thickness of the fillets.

5. Drain the noodles well and toss in a little cooking oil. Pile onto plates and place the fish on top, pouring the sauce.

Variation
* Use Japanese rice vinegar or dry sherry in place of fish stock or water.

Piperade with Fresh Noodles

The combination of tomatoes, red peppers and eggs is a typical dish of Southern France, where it is usually served with crusty French bread. However, it also works very well with fresh noodles.

I large red pepper, seeded and quartered

I tablespoon olive oil

½ small onion, peeled and sliced

I small clove garlic, peeled and crushed (optional)

2 tomatoes, peeled and coarsely chopped

I bayleaf

dash of Tabasco sauce

225-300g / 8-10oz fresh noodles

salt

3 eggs

I tablespoon water

freshly ground black pepper

sprigs of fresh parsley

1. Grill the red pepper until the skin blisters. Leave to cool a little and peel. Cut into thin strips.

2. Heat the oil in a large heavy frying pan and fry the onion and garlic, if using, for 3-4 minutes until lightly browned.

3. Add the red pepper, tomatoes, bayleaf and Tabasco and cook over a low heat for 12-15 minutes, stirring from time to time.

4. Meanwhile, plunge the noodles into a large saucepan of boiling salted water and cook for 2-3 minutes until just tender. Drain and toss in a little oil. Keep warm.

5. Beat the eggs with the water and black pepper and pour into the pan of red pepper. Gently stir the mixture over medium heat until the eggs are just beginning to set. Add the noodles and toss well together.

6. Serve at once, garnished with sprigs of fresh parsley.

Hungarian Tokany
with Flat Noodles

This is a very quick paprika stew which tastes rather like a spicier version of beef stroganoff. In Hungary it would be served with long flat noodles which are about 1cm / ½in wide. However, any kind of long flat noodles, such as tagliatelle, can be used.

I tablespoon cooking oil

50g / 2oz smoked bacon, cut into thin strips

I onion, peeled and sliced

225g / 8oz frying rump or sirloin steak, cut into thin strips

½ tablespoon paprika pepper

½ teaspoon cornflour

150ml / ¼ pint soured cream

salt and freshly ground black pepper

225-300g / 8-10oz fresh flat noodles

small knob of butter

1. Heat half the cooking oil in a large frying pan and fry the bacon for 1 minute. Add the onion and fry for about 4-5 minutes until very lightly browned. Remove from the pan and keep on one side.

2. Add the remaining cooking oil to the pan and fry the steak until sealed all over. Mix the paprika pepper and cornflour with a tablespoon of soured cream and stir into the beef, then add the bacon and onion mixture and the rest of the cream. Season and stir.

3. Gently bring to the boil and simmer for 10-15 minutes until the beef is cooked and tender.

4. Plunge the noodles into a large saucepan of boiling salted water and cook for 2-3 minutes until just tender. Drain well and toss in the butter.

5. Spoon the noodles onto plates and top with the Tokany sauce.

Italian Noodles
with Bacon Sauce

By cooking over a medium to high heat, the punchy flavours of this spicy sauce can be achieved in about the same time as it takes to cook the noodles, but you need to stir regularly to stop it sticking to the pan.

I buy bacon off-cuts at a local store which sells unwrapped bacon. The mix may include smoked and unsmoked bacon and gammon; it makes a very economical buy.

2 tablespoons olive oil

175g / 6oz trimmed bacon bits, diced

1 small onion, peeled and finely chopped

1-2 cloves garlic, peeled and crushed

1 x 400g / 14oz can chopped tomatoes or 450g / 1lb skinned and chopped fresh tomatoes

2 teaspoons tomato purée

75g / 3oz black olives stoned

salt and freshly ground black pepper

225g / 8oz dried Italian noodles of your choice

freshly chopped basil, parsley and thyme

1. Heat the olive oil in a deep saucepan. Add the bacon and fry for a couple of minutes. Next add the onion and garlic and continue frying and stirring until lightly browned.

2. Add the contents of the can of tomatoes or the fresh tomatoes. Stir and bring to the boil. Add all the remaining ingredients, except the noodles, and stir again.

3. Set the heat to medium and allow the mixture to boil fairly fast for about 10-15 minutes, stirring regularly.

4. Cook the Italian noodles in lightly salted boiling water for about 8-10 minutes or for the length of time given on the pack. Drain well.

5. Pour the sauce over the noodles and toss well together. Serve at once sprinkled with freshly chopped herbs.

Oriental Meatballs
with Chinese Noodles

This makes a good meal served with a green salad. Alternatively, you could add extra vegetables to the tossed noodles to make the dish more substantial.

2 tablespoons cooking oil

¼ teaspoon whole coriander seeds

¼ teaspoon whole cumin seeds

I clove garlic, peeled and crushed

½ small onion, peeled and very finely chopped

225g / 8oz lean minced beef

2 teaspoons garam masala or curry powder or paste

½ x 250g / 9oz pack dried egg noodles

I bunch spring onions, trimmed and cut into 1cm / ½in lengths

50ml / 2fl oz beef stock made with ¼ beef stock cube and boiling water

a few drops Tabasco sauce

125g / 4oz beansprouts

1. Heat half the oil in a small heavy-based pan and fry the whole spices for half a minute. Add the garlic and onion. Fry for 3-4 minutes over a medium heat until lightly browned.

2. Put the meat in a bowl and add the fried onions and spices, discarding any liquid fat. Add the curry powder or paste and mix well.

3. Shape the mixture into 14 small balls and dry fry in a non-stick frying pan for 5-6 minutes until cooked through.

4. Plunge the noodles into boiling water and cook or leave to stand for the length of time given on the pack.

5. Heat the remaining oil in a wok or deep frying pan and stir-fry the spring onions for a minute. Drain the noodles and add to the pan with the stock and Tabasco. Toss over a medium heat and add the beansprouts. Serve at once with the meatballs spooned on top.

Orange and Cardamom
Chicken Wings on Fresh Noodles

Chicken wings always look like an economical buy in the supermarket but what does one do with them? This adaptation of an Eastern idea provides one answer. Serve with steamed broccoli on the side.

4-6 chicken wings

I tablespoon cooking oil

I clove garlic, peeled and crushed

grated rind and juice of I orange

juice of ½ lemon

50ml / 2fl oz white wine or chicken stock

seeds from 3 cardamom pods, crushed

salt and freshly ground black pepper

225g / 8oz fresh noodles

I level teaspoon cornflour

I tablespoon water

sprigs of fresh parsley or spring onion flowers

1. Cut off the wing tops and remove a little of the excess skin on the joint.

2. Heat the oil in a frying pan and quickly brown the wings.

3. Transfer the wings to a saucepan. Add the garlic, orange rind and juice, lemon juice, wine or stock, cardamom seeds and seasoning. Bring to the boil and simmer for 10-12 minutes, turning the wings in the liquid from time to time.

4. Plunge the noodles into a large saucepan of boiling water and cook for 2-3 minutes until just tender. Drain and toss in a little oil.

5. Remove the chicken wings from the saucepan and keep warm. Mix the cornflour with the tablespoon of water and blend into the liquid in the pan. Bring to the boil and cook for 1 minute.

6. Pile the noodles onto plates. Top with the chicken wings and pour on the sauce. Garnish with sprigs of parsley or spring onion flowers.

Devilled Kidneys
with Fresh Noodles

*I discovered that this classic English recipe works far better with noodles
than it ever did with rice or potatoes. Look for the widest noodles you can
find and layer the sauce between the strands when you serve it out. This
looks attractive and allows the noodles to take up some of the sauce.*

I small onion, peeled and finely chopped

I tablespoon cooking oil

4-6 lamb kidneys, skinned and cut into pieces

75g / 3oz button mushrooms, cut into quarters

I tablespoon plain flour

salt and freshly ground black pepper

½-I teaspoon made mustard

½ teaspoon Worcestershire sauce

pinch of dried thyme

75ml / 3fl oz red wine or strong beef stock

225-300g / 8-10oz fresh noodles

sprigs of fresh parsley

1. Fry the onions in the cooking oil for 2-3 minutes until soft, but not
brown. Add the kidneys and cook for a further minute, stirring from
time to time.

2. Add the mushrooms, flour and seasoning and stir well. Add all the
remaining ingredients, except the noodles and parsley, and bring to
the boil, stirring all the time. Reduce the heat and simmer for 10-12
minutes, stirring from time to time.

3. Plunge the noodles into a large saucepan of boiling salted water and
cook for 2-3 minutes until just tender.

4. Spoon the noodles onto individual dishes, layering with the kidneys
and mushrooms. Serve at once, garnished with sprigs of parsley.

FRIED NOODLE DISHES

Noodles can be fried in three different ways depending on the type of noodle. Almost all noodles can be stir-fried with a variety of ingredients to make substantial dishes such as Singapore Noodles (see page 90) and Indonesian Bah Mee (see page 80). These are filling enough to form a meal in themselves with a salad on the side.

Egg and wheat noodles (but not rice noodles) can be fried in a solid mass to make a crispy base for other stir-fry mixtures. I sometimes make these in a small 15cm / 6in frying pan as individual bases which look very attractive. However, if you only have one such pan, this takes rather longer to do than making a single base and cutting it into wedges.

Finally, rice or bean flour noodles (but not egg or wheat noodles) can be deep-fried in hot cooking oil. They puff up to a crispy mass three or four times their original size. It is fun to make individual nests of crispy noodles by using a small (15cm / 6in) deep-sided pan. Because of the increase in volume they must be cooked in very small batches.

To deep fry noodles, fill a third of the way up the sides of the pan with cooking oil and place on a medium heat. Test to see if the fat is at the right temperature by dropping a small piece of noodle into the oil. It should crisp up immediately. Plunge the noodles into the hot oil in small batches (about 25g / 1oz loose bundle) and hold down under the boiling oil. Care must be taken not to use too much oil or too many noodles otherwise the oil will boil over which is extremely dangerous.

Check that the hot oil has penetrated each bundle to the centre. If it has not, the noodles in the middle will be very hard and brittle and will need to be removed or another batch cooked.

Deep-fried crispy noodles can be served with hot or cold toppings or be used themselves as a crispy topping for other dishes.

NB: Crispy noodles must be prepared immediately before they are required, as they tend to go stale very quickly; this is particularly so in the case of noodles made from bean flour.

Noodle
Tortilla Squares

If you can use starchy potatoes in Spanish tortilla, I asked myself, why not use noodles? The only way to answer this was to try it out. I was very pleased with the results. The tortilla squares can be served hot or cold, so make double quantity and add them to packed lunches or picnic boxes.

1 x 90g / 3½oz Japanese wholewheat ramen noodles

2 tablespoons cooking oil

1 small onion, peeled and chopped

1 small red or green pepper, seeded and chopped

4 large eggs, beaten

salt and freshly ground black pepper

2 tablespoons water

1. Plunge the noodles into a large saucepan of boiling water and cook or leave to stand for the length of time given on the pack. (Keep the soup stock mix to enhance a soup recipe later in the week.) Drain the noodles very well.

2. Heat the cooking oil in a small frying pan and gently fry the vegetables for 2-3 minutes. Do not allow them to brown. Roughly chop the drained noodles and mix with the vegetables in the pan.

3. Beat together the eggs, seasoning and water and pour over the vegetables and noodles. Cook over a medium heat for 4 minutes until lightly browned underneath.

4. Slide onto a large plate and return to the pan the other side up. Cook for a further 2-4 minutes.

5. Cut into squares to serve.

Variation

* Use cooked peas or sweetcorn kernels in place of the peppers.

Chicken Chow Mein

Unlike Chop Suey this really is an authentic Chinese dish, but it became really popular in California when the Chinese were cooking for the rail workers. No US, or indeed UK, Chinese restaurant is now without a recipe for this continual favourite.

3 tablespoons cooking oil

I chicken breast fillet, boned, skinned and shredded

I onion, peeled and sliced

50g / 2oz mushrooms, sliced

½ green or red pepper, seeded and shredded

½ can Chinese vegetables, such as bamboo shoots or water chestnuts (optional)

salt and freshly ground black pepper

I teaspoon cornflour

100ml / 4fl oz chicken stock or dry white wine

75g / 3oz Chinese greens, sliced

½ x 250g / 9oz pack dried egg noodles

pinch of five spice powder

2 teaspoons soy sauce

1. Heat a third of the oil in a deep frying pan or wok and stir-fry the chicken for 2-3 minutes. Check to see that there is no pinkness in the centre of the chicken. Remove from the pan and keep on one side.

2. Add another third of the oil to the pan and stir-fry all the vegetables, except the greens, for 3-4 minutes. Add seasoning.

3. Mix the cornflour and a little of the chicken stock or white wine to a smooth paste. Stir in the rest of the stock or wine and pour over the vegetables.

4. Add the Chinese greens, bring the mixture to the boil and simmer for 5 minutes. Stir in the chicken pieces.

5. Plunge the noodles into a large saucepan of boiling water and cook or leave to stand for the time given on the pack.

6. Heat the remaining oil in another wok or deep frying pan. Drain the noodles and transfer to the frying pan. Add the soy sauce and five spice powder and stir-fry over a high heat for one minute.

7. Pile the noodles onto individual plates and top with the chicken and vegetable mixture.

Variations

* Shredded pork fillet can be used in place of chicken. If this is too expensive, buy spare rib chops and cut out the bones.

* Stir-fry bean shoots or spring onions with the noodles.

Spiced Beef
with
Fried Chilli Noodles

This is a real mid-week stand-by. It is quick and easy to make and does not need too many ingredients. Serve with a mixed leaf salad and finish with fruit and cheese.

½ x 250g / 9oz pack of chilli-flavoured noodles

3 tablespoons cooking oil

I teaspoon whole coriander seeds

I small onion, peeled and finely chopped

I clove garlic, peeled and crushed

225g/8oz lean minced beef

I teaspoon dried oregano

225g / 8oz broccoli, roughly chopped

50ml / 2fl oz beef stock

I teaspoon soy sauce

freshly ground black pepper

1. Plunge the noodles into a large saucepan of boiling water and cook or leave to stand for the time given on the pack.

2. Heat half the cooking oil in a wok or deep frying pan and fry the whole coriander seeds for about 1 minute until they start to pop. Add the onion and garlic and fry for 2-3 minutes until the onion turns transparent.

3. Next add the minced beef and herbs and cook until lightly browned and quite broken up or grainy. Remove from the pan, draining off all excess fat. Keep warm.

4. Heat the remaining cooking oil in the frying pan or wok and stir-fry the broccoli for 2 minutes. Drain the noodles, add to the pan and stir-fry for a further 1-2 minutes.

5. Pour on the beef stock and bring to the boil. Add the cooked beef and seasoning then cook for 1 minute. Serve at once with a sprinkling of soy sauce.

Variation
* Add 1 small red pepper, seeded and finely chopped, with the onion and garlic.

Indonesian Bah Mee

For special occasions the Indonesians add shredded barbecued pork to the egg and spring onion garnishes - you may be able to buy this from your local Chinese restaurant or take-away. It is known as Char Siu and is usually a pork fillet which has been marinated in a bright red mix of spices and herbs.

I egg

I tablespoon water

salt and freshly ground black pepper

2 tablespoons cooking oil

I bunch spring onions

½ x 250g / 9oz pack dried egg noodles

125g / 4oz bacon bits, trimmed and diced

300g / 10oz mixed stir-fry vegetables, including beansprouts

3 tablespoons dried coconut milk powder

75g / 3oz cooked peeled prawns

2 tablespoons soy sauce

3-4 tablespoons water or white wine

1. Beat the egg with the water and seasoning. Heat a little of the oil in a small frying pan. Pour on the egg mixture and allow it to spread thinly across the base of the pan. Cook for a minute or so until set and lightly browned underneath. Turn over and lightly brown the second side. Remove from the pan and leave to cool. Cut into strips.

2. Trim the spring onions and slice the stems of four of them back to the bulb two or three times. Place in a cup of water to make spring onion flowers. Coarsely chop the remaining onions.

3. Plunge the dried egg noodles into a saucepan of boiling water. Cook or leave to stand for the length of time given on the pack.

4. Stir-fry the bacon in the rest of the cooking oil in a non-stick wok or deep frying pan. Add the chopped spring onions and mixed vegetables and stir-fry for a further 2 minutes.

5. Drain the noodles, pat dry on kitchen paper and add to the vegetables with the all the remaining ingredients. Mix everything well together by tossing over a high heat for about 1 minut?.

6. Spoon into bowls, garnish with the prepared strips of egg and the spring onion flowers and serve at once.

Variations

* Use left-over cooked meats such as chicken, pork or ham in place of bacon bits.

* Most supermarkets sell ready-mixed packs of stir-fry vegetables but if you cannot find a pack, make up your own mix using a selection of beansprouts, sliced peppers, Chinese leaves, baby corn, mushrooms, celery, beans, mangetout or whatever you have to hand.

* If you cannot find dried coconut milk use about 25g / 1oz creamed coconut dissolved in a little water instead.

Quick Barbecued Chicken
on a
Crispy Noodle Base

In this delicious dish, the sweet chilli sauce gives a wonderful flavour to the chicken without any need for you to make a basting mixture. Serve with a side salad of watercress and cucumber tossed in a sesame vinaigrette.

½ x 250g / 9oz pack dried wheat or egg noodles

2 chicken breast fillets, skinned and boned

I teaspoon sesame oil

2 tablespoons Chinese sweet chilli sauce

2 tablespoons cooking oil

I small onion, peeled and thinly sliced

3-4 sprigs fresh coriander coarsely chopped

I tablespoon toasted sesame seeds

soy sauce, to serve

1. Plunge the noodles into a large saucepan of boiling water and cook or leave to stand for the length of time given on the pack.

2. Flatten the chicken breasts by placing them between sheets of clingfilm and beating with a rolling pin. Brush each side with a little sesame oil.

3. Place on a grill tray and spread half the chilli sauce over the top. Grill for 4-5 minutes. Turn over and spread the remaining sauce over the second side. Grill for another 3 minutes until the chicken is fully cooked through and there is no sign of pinkness in the flesh.

4. Drain and dry the noodles. Heat half the cooking oil in a small frying pan and add the noodles. Press well down into the pan and cook over a medium heat for 5 minutes until the noodles are crisp and golden underneath.

5. Slide the mass of noodles onto a flat plate in one piece. Return to the pan the other way up and cook for a further 5 minutes until crisp.

6. Heat the remaining cooking oil in a small frying pan and fry the onion for 3-4 minutes until brown and crisp. Drain on kitchen paper. Mix with the chopped coriander and sesame seeds.

7. Slide the cooked noodles onto a serving plate. Slice the chicken and place on the top. Sprinkle with the onion, coriander and sesame mixture and serve at once with soy sauce on the side.

Variation

* Use one of the many Chinese barbecue sauces now on sale in the supermarkets instead of the sweet chilli sauce.

Noodle Pancakes
with
Florentine Eggs

These pancakes are quite filling but not at all heavy to eat. They make a very unusual quick meal to serve at any time of the day. Top with scrambled eggs and smoked salmon trimmings for breakfast or brunch, with bacon and mushroom stir-fry for lunch, or with this Italian-style egg and spinach topping for supper.

½ x 90g / 3½oz pack Japanese wholewheat ramen or noodles

75g / 3oz plain flour

I egg, beaten

150ml / 5fl oz milk

I teaspoon baking powder

salt and freshly ground black pepper

450g / 1lb fresh leaf spinach or small pack of frozen leaf spinach

¼ teaspoon ground nutmeg

2 tablespoons water

knob of butter

3-4 eggs, beaten

I tablespoon cooking oil

1. Plunge the noodles into a saucepan of boiling water and cook for the length of time given on the pack. Drain and dry on kitchen paper. (Keep the dried stock pack for another recipe.)

2. Meanwhile, make the pancake batter by mixing the flour with the single beaten egg and the milk. Stir the prepared noodles into the batter with the baking powder and seasoning.

3. If using fresh spinach, wash the leaves, place in a pan with no extra water and cook over a low heat until completely wilted. Drain in a

sieve and toss with nutmeg. If using frozen spinach, heat through, drain well and toss with nutmeg. Keep warm.

4. Heat the water and butter in a small saucepan and pour in the remaining eggs. Scramble by stirring with a fork or wooden spoon until the eggs are lightly cooked. Keep warm.

5. Heat the oil in a heavy frying pan. Stir the batter mixture and spoon half of it into the pan. Make sure that the noodles are spread throughout the pancake.

6. Cook for 2-3 minutes until the pancake has risen and is lightly browned on the base. Turn over and cook the other side for another minute or so. Keep warm and repeat with the remaining batter.

7. Place the pancakes on warm plates. Spread the cooked spinach over the pancakes and top with scrambled eggs. Serve at once.

Crispy Rice Noodles
with
Chicken in Yellow Bean Sauce

*Serve this quick stand-by with stir-fried or lightly steamed vegetables. If
you are particularly hungry, start the meal with toast and pâté or
Bruschetta made with garlic, olive oil, chopped tomatoes and fresh herbs on
Ciabatta or French bread.*

cooking oil

125g / 4oz rice vermicelli

2 chicken breast fillets or a breast and a thigh, skinned and boned

½ small onion, peeled and sliced

1 clove garlic, peeled and crushed

2 tablespoons yellow bean sauce

1 teaspoon rice or wine vinegar

1 teaspoon sugar

2 tablespoons chicken stock

1 egg, lightly beaten

50g / 2oz small cooked and peeled prawns (optional)

1. Start by deep frying the vermicelli in small batches. Heat oil in a wok
or very deep frying pan, then drop a small piece of dry noodle into the
fat to see if it is ready. It should puff up immediately.

2. Drop a small bundle of noodles into the fat. Remove with a perforated
spoon as soon as it is crisp and dry on kitchen paper. Repeat with the
remaining bundle of noodles. Keep the fried noodles in a warm place.

3. Cut the breast fillets into evenly sized strips.

4. Heat 1 tablespoon oil in a wok or shallow-sided frying pan and stir-
fry the onion and garlic for 1 minute. Add the chicken and continue
stir-frying for 2 minutes. Pour on the bean sauce, vinegar, sugar and
stock and bring to the boil. Reduce heat, cover and simmer.

5. Heat a little more oil in a small frying pan and pour in the beaten egg. Allow it to spread out thinly over the base. Cook until set and then dice.

6. Toss into the chicken mixture with the prawns, if using. Heat through and serve on top of the crispy noodles.

Variation
* Toasted cashews are very good used in place of the prawns. Allow about 25-35g / 1-1½oz.

Crunchy Fried Rice Sticks
with
Stir-fried Pork

Rice based tagliatelle is easier to deal with than the thin rice vermicelli. It crisps up in just the same way but the batches are easier to separate and handle.

cooking oil

125g / 4oz rice vermicelli or rice tagliatelle

225g / 8oz very lean pork meat, cut into thin slices

2 level teaspoons cornflour

salt and freshly ground black pepper

1 tablespoon chopped fresh root ginger

1 clove garlic, peeled and chopped

4 spring onions, trimmed and finely chopped

125g / 4oz carrots, sliced on the slant

125g / 4oz courgettes, sliced on the slant

50g / 2oz mangetout, trimmed

75ml / 3fl oz pork stock made with boiling water and 1 pork stock cube

2 teaspoons soy sauce

1. Start by deep frying the rice noodles in small batches. Heat the oil in a wok or very deep frying pan. Drop a small piece of dry noodle into the fat to see if it is ready. It should puff up immediately.

2. Drop a small bundle of noodles into the fat. Remove with a perforated spoon as soon as it is crisp and dry on kitchen paper. Repeat with the remaining bundle of noodles. Keep the fried noodles in a warm place.

3. Toss the pork in cornflour and seasoning. Heat 3 tablespoons of cooking oil in a deep frying pan or wok and stir-fry the ginger, garlic and onion for 1 minute. Add the pork and stir-fry for 2-3 minutes until cooked through. Remove from the pan and keep warm.

4. Add another 2 tablespoons of cooking oil to the pan and stir-fry the carrots for 1 minute, then add the courgettes and mangetout and continue stir-frying for a further minute.

5. Return the pork to the pan and pour on the stock and soy sauce. Bring to the boil and cook over a high heat for another minute or so, tossing the vegetables in the sauce.

6. Serve with the crispy noodles.

Variation

* Use Chinese vegetables such as water chestnuts and bamboo shoots in place of courgettes and mangetout.

* Add some fine spice powder for a more aromatic dish.

Singapore Noodles

This dish may be made with thin dried egg noodles or with rice noodles. It is very good served with other Chinese dishes, or makes a meal in itself if you increase the quantities of ham or pork.

½ x 250g / 9oz pack dried egg noodles

2 tablespoons cooking oil

I tablespoon curry powder

I small onion, peeled and thinly sliced

4-5 drops Tabasco sauce

4 tablespoons light soy sauce

50g / 2oz beansprouts

¼ green pepper, seeded and cut into slivers

¼ red pepper, seeded and cut into slivers

50g / 2oz small cooked and peeled prawns (optional)

50g / 2oz cooked ham or barbecued pork, finely diced

sprigs of fresh broadleaf parsley or spring onion flowers

1. Plunge the noodles into a saucepan of boiling water. Cook or leave to stand for the time given on the pack.

2. Heat the oil in a large frying pan or wok. Add the curry powder and the onion to the pan and stir-fry for 1 minute.

3. Add all the remaining ingredients, except the parsley or spring onion flowers, and bring to the boil.

4. Drain the noodles very well and add to the pan of vegetables. Toss well over a medium heat for 1 minute and serve garnished with parsley or spring onion flowers.

Caribbean Crispy Noodles
with Greens

When slavery was abolished in the Caribbean Islands, a large number of Chinese came to the islands to work on the sugar cane plantations. The Chinese settlers adapted the local ingredients to their own cuisine and this is one of the resulting recipes, based on traditional Chow Mein.

½ x 250g / 9oz pack of dried egg noodles

2 tablespoons cooking oil

I onion, peeled and sliced

125g / 4oz greens (cabbage, kale, bok choy or
spring greens), coarsely shredded

I dessertspoon soy sauce

50g / 2oz beansprouts

125g / 4oz cooked ham, gammon or pork, cut into strips

freshly ground black pepper

1. Plunge the noodles into a large saucepan of boiling water and cook or leave to stand for the length of time given on the pack.

2. Heat half the cooking oil in a frying pan or wok and stir-fry the onion and greens for 3-4 minutes until cooked to your taste.

3. Drain and dry the noodles. Heat the remaining oil in a small frying pan and add the noodles. Press well down into the pan and cook over a medium heat for 5 minutes until the noodles are crisp and golden underneath.

4. Slide the mass of noodles onto a flat plate in one piece. Return to the pan the other way up and cook for a further minute until crisp.

5. Add the soy sauce, beansprouts and meat to the stir-fried vegetables and toss over a medium heat for 2 minutes. Season with black pepper.

6. Slip the fried noodles onto a serving plate and top with the vegetable mixture.

BAKED NOODLE DISHES

The dishes in this section take a little longer than those in the other sections of the book. Allow around 40-45 minutes for both preparation and cooking. One or two of the recipes, such as the foil baked noodles, will take a little less time.

Each recipe makes a complete course in itself. Start the meal with a soup or salad and finish with fruit.

Baked Noodles with Eggs

This unusual dish from Northern Italy is not quite a soufflé, but it is very light. Start the meal with Minestrone or vegetable soup and serve this dish with steamed green beans.

50g-75g / 2-3oz dried egg noodles

4 eggs

salt and freshly ground black pepper

2 tablespoons plain white flour

2 tablespoons white wine or water

25g / 1oz butter

1 large continental tomato, sliced

50g / 2oz breadcrumbs

125g / 4oz mozzarella, sliced

1. Heat the oven to 220C/425F/Gas 7.

2. Plunge the noodles into a saucepan of boiling water. Cook or leave to stand for the length of time given on the pack. Drain and dry.

3. Beat the eggs with seasoning, flour and wine or water. Stir in the noodles.

4. Heat half the butter in a frying pan and pour in the egg mixture. Cook until the underside is just set.

5. Transfer to a dish of the same size and top with the tomatoes, breadcrumbs and cheese. Dot with the remaining butter and bake for 15 minutes.

Variation
* Toss the noodles with fresh herbs before adding to the eggs.

Foil Baked Noodles
in
Spicy Sauce

The idea for this fragrant parcel of Italian noodles came from a recent visit to the Val d'Aosta in the north west corner of Italy. There Fontina cheese is baked with tomatoes, garlic and spaghetti in just such a foil parcel. I have not used Fontina in this recipe as it is almost impossible to buy here but you can sprinkle grated Parmesan cheese over the dish when it is opened up.

225g / 8oz dried fettucine or thin flat noodles

salt

2 tablespoons olive oil

2 cloves garlic, peeled and crushed

1 small fresh chilli, seeded and finely chopped

500g / 1lb ripe tomatoes, peeled and diced

1 tablespoon tomato purée

12-14 stoned black olives

1 tablespoon capers (optional)

freshly ground black pepper

2 tablespoons freshly chopped coriander

freshly grated Parmesan cheese

1. Heat the oven to 200C/400F/Gas 6. Line a small baking tin with foil, leaving plenty of foil to fold over the top.

2. Half cook the noodles in plenty of lightly salted boiling water for about 3-5 minutes depending on the directions on the pack.

3. Heat the oil in a saucepan and fry the garlic and chilli for 2-3 minutes. Add the tomatoes, tomato purée, olives and capers and cook for 10 minutes over a medium heat, stirring all the time. Season with black pepper.

Oriental Seafood Soup *(page 21)*

Variation on Quick Tossed Vegetable Noodles *(page 40)*

Italian Noodles with Bacon Sauce *(page 69)*

Noodle Pancakes with Florentine Eggs *(page 84)*

Variation on Simple Stir-fried Noodles *(page 107)*

Cold Tossed Noodles with Cucumber Sesame Sauce *(page 122)*

Crunchy Salsa with Deep Fried Noodles *(page 126)*

Hot Tossed Apricot and Almond Noodles *(page 131)*

4. Drain the noodles well and place in the foil-lined tin. Top with the sauce.

5. Close up the foil, leaving a fairly large space above the noodles so that the steam may circulate inside the foil parcel. Bake for about 10 minutes until the pasta is just cooked.

6. Open up the parcel at the table and sprinkle with the chopped coriander. Serve from the foil with a bowl of freshly grated Parmesan cheese.

Variations

* Add diced aubergines to the sauce with the tomatoes.

* Add ½ small can of drained and washed anchovies to the sauce with the tomatoes.

* Add a pack of mixed cooked shellfish just before the parcels go into the oven.

Eastern Style
Noodles in Foil

Another variation on the foil parcel theme, I sometimes serve this dish with grilled or fried Teryaki-marinated chicken or pork escalopes.

175g / 6oz dried fettucine or Italian noodles

salt

1 tablespoon cooking oil

2 cloves garlic, peeled and chopped

1 bunch spring onions, trimmed and cut into chunky lengths

1 tablespoon freshly grated root ginger (or in oil)

¼ teaspoon five spice powder

1 teaspoon ground lemon grass in oil or 1 large whole stick of lemon grass cut into 5cm / 2in pieces

2 tablespoons powdered coconut milk

150ml / ¼ pint water

1. Heat the oven to 190C/375F/Gas 5. Line a small baking tin with foil, leaving plenty of foil to fold over the top.

2. Half cook the fettucine or noodles in plenty of lightly salted boiling water for 3-5 minutes depending on the directions on the pack.

3. Heat the oil in a pan and gently fry the garlic, spring onions and ginger for 2-3 minutes. Stir in the five spice powder and lemon grass.

4. Mix the dried coconut milk and water and pour over the fried vegetables.

5. Drain the noodles well and place on the foil. Top with the coconut milk mixture.

6. Close up the foil, leaving a fairly large space above the noodles so that the steam may circulate inside the foil parcel. Bake for about 10-15 minutes until the pasta is just cooked. Serve from the foil at table.

Variations

Add with the coconut milk mixture one or more of the following ingredients to make a more substantial dish:

* 125g / 4oz cooked and shredded chicken meat
* 75g / 3oz shredded Chinese leaves or Swiss chard
* 50g / 2oz mangetout, sugar peas or shelled peas

Sicilian Baked Noodles with Aubergines

Aubergines are extremely popular in the island of Sicily and they turn up in all kind of dishes. This one has an interesting mixture of textures, with the soft aubergines, firm noodles and crispy cheese topping.

2 tablespoons olive or cooking oil

2 cloves garlic, peeled and crushed

50g / 2 oz diced bacon bits

I x 225g / 8oz can chopped tomatoes

300g / 10oz aubergine, diced

I red pepper, seeded and chopped

¼ teaspoon dried oregano

freshly ground black pepper

125g / 4oz fresh Italian noodles or Japanese wheat noodles

salt

50g / 2oz grated cheese

50g / 2oz fresh breadcrumbs

15g / ½oz butter

1. Heat the oven to 220C/425F/Gas 7.

2. Heat the oil in a small pan and fry the garlic and bacon until lightly browned. Add the tomatoes, aubergine, pepper, oregano and black pepper and bring to the boil. Cook over a medium heat for 10 minutes to thicken a little.

3. Half cook the fresh Italian noodles in plenty of lightly salted boiling water for 1-2 minutes or cook the Japanese noodles for the time given on the pack.

4. Grease a baking dish and layer the noodles with the sauce in the dish. Top with the cheese and breadcrumbs mixed together. Dot with butter. Bake for 15 minutes until lightly browned on top.

Variation
* Add a spoonful of stoned black olives.

Pasticcio

You will find versions of this dish all over the Eastern Mediterranean. In Southern Italy aubergines and tomatoes form the base of the sauce. In Greece and Turkey minced lamb is an important ingredient. This particular version comes from Bari near Puglia in the heel of Italy.

75g / 3oz Italian flat noodles broken into 7cm / 3in lengths

salt

I teaspoon olive oil

I x 225g / 8oz can tomatoes

I clove garlic, peeled and crushed

I tablespoon tomato purée

2-3 sticks celery, very finely chopped

2 leeks, trimmed and finely chopped

salt and freshly ground black pepper

125g / 4oz chicken livers, cut into pieces

15g / ½oz butter

15g / ½oz flour

100ml / 4fl oz milk

50g / 2oz mature Cheddar cheese, grated

1. Heat the oven to 200C/400F/Gas 6 and grease a pie dish.

2. Cook the noodles in lightly salted boiling water for 8-10 minutes or for the length of time given on the pack.

3. Empty the contents of the can of tomatoes into a saucepan and add the garlic, tomato purée, celery, leeks and seasoning and bring to the boil. Cook for 10 minutes until fairly thick. Add the chicken livers and cook for a further 5 minutes, stirring from time to time.

4. Drain the noodles and mix with the sauce. Grease a pie dish and pour the noodle mixture into the dish.

5. Place the butter, flour and milk in a pan and bring to the boil, stirring with a wire whisk. When the mixture thickens add the cheese and pour over the noodles. Bake for 20 minutes.

Baked Noodles
with Blue Cheese
and Parsley

This is a Texan-style version of Macaroni Cheese but it is much lighter and fluffier. It is also a good deal tastier. Serve with a tossed green salad and finish the meal with juicy pineapple and mangoes.

175g / 6oz fresh noodles, cut into short lengths

50g / 2oz melted butter

1 x 175g / 6oz fromage frais

4 tablespoons freshly chopped parsley

1 clove garlic, peeled and crushed

1 small onion, peeled and grated

50g / 2oz blue cheese, crumbled

salt and freshly ground black pepper

3 eggs, beaten

paprika pepper

1. Heat the oven to 195C/375F/Gas 5.

2. Plunge the noodles into a large saucepan of salted boiling water and cook for 2-3 minutes until just tender.

3. Drain the noodles, then mix with all the ingredients, except the paprika, and pour into a greased casserole or pie dish.

4. Bake for 45 minutes until just set in the centre. Sprinkle with paprika pepper and serve at once.

Variation

* You can also use fresh or dried spinach noodles which gives the dish a very pretty green colour.

Souffléd Tomato Noodles with Olives

The idea for this combination of olives and dill comes from the South of France. The result is both tasty and unusual.

50g / 2oz fresh tomato noodles

salt and freshly ground black pepper

4 eggs

1 tablespoon plain flour

2 tablespoons milk

125g / 4oz grated Cheddar cheese

25g / 1oz stoned black olives, chopped

1 tablespoon freshly chopped or frozen dill

1. Heat the oven to 190C/375F/Gas 5.

2. Cook the noodles in plenty of lightly salted boiling water for 2-3 minutes until just cooked. Drain well and pat dry with kitchen paper. Cut into lengths.

3. Beat the eggs with the seasonings. Mix the flour and milk to a paste and whisk into the eggs with a wire whisk.

4. Stir in the cheese and olives, cooked noodles and dill. Pour the mixture into a greased soufflé dish and bake for 45-50 minutes.

Variations

* Substitute diced ham and parsley for the olives and dill.

* Use Brie, Camembert or goat's cheese in place of Cheddar. You may need to cut the quantities a little with very strong cheeses.

Baked Egg Noodles
with Fish

The soft, creamy textures of this dish are well complemented with simple green peas.

50g / 2oz dried egg noodles

225g / 8oz white fish fillets (plaice, haddock, huss or whiting)

salt and freshly ground black pepper

½ teaspoon ground nutmeg

2 tablespoons freshly chopped parsley

2 eggs, beaten

100ml / 4fl oz milk

1. Heat the oven to 190C/375F/Gas 5.

2. Plunge the noodles into a large saucepan of boiling water and cook or leave to stand for the length of time given on the pack. Drain well and chop coarsely.

3. Layer the chopped noodles with the fish fillets in a greased baking dish, seasoning and sprinkling the layers with nutmeg and parsley. Beat the eggs with the milk and pour over the top.

4. Bake for 40-45 minutes until golden on top and set in the centre.

Variation
* Add 3 tablespoons soft cheese to the egg and milk mixture. If you do this you could leave out one of the eggs.

NOODLES
ON THE SIDE

Noodles can accompany many different types of food. Indeed in some countries they are used in much the same way as you might use potatoes or rice. They are often served in this way in Eastern Europe. In the Far East, too, they are served as a filler with other dishes.

If the accompanying main dish is quite runny or has a rich sauce, serve the noodles with a simple knob of butter or a trickle of oil. With drier main dishes, such as roasts and grills, the noodles can be much more interesting without clashing with the other food.

In this section I have put together a collection of noodle dishes which are suitable for serving on the side.

Simple
Stir-fried Noodles

In China and many parts of the Far East, noodles are simply flavoured with ginger, spring onions and perhaps soy sauce to make a quick accompaniment for all manner of stir-fries. This dish is also very good served with grills, barbecues and even casseroles which have an oriental flavour to them.

½ x 250g / 9oz pack dried egg or wheat noodles

2 tablespoons cooking oil

½ bunch spring onions, trimmed and cut into lengths

I cm / ½ in piece fresh root ginger, peeled and grated

freshly ground black pepper

I tablespoon soy sauce (optional)

1. Plunge the noodles into a large saucepan of boiling water and cook or leave to stand for the time given on the pack.

2. Heat the oil in a wok or deep frying pan and stir-fry the onions and ginger for 1 minute.

3. Drain the noodles well and add to the pan of onions and ginger. Add pepper and soy sauce, if using, and toss over a low heat. Serve at once.

Variations

* Add a little garlic to the mixture in the pan.

* If you are serving Thai food, use lemon grass instead of either the spring onion or the ginger.

* Add seasonal vegetables such as carrots and mangetout or mouli and beans, as available.

Stir-fried Noodles
with
Beansprouts

This is another Eastern standby which marries very well with most dishes. Rather surprisingly, it makes a good background for barbecued food, particularly if you have plenty of pickles and relishes on hand.

½ x 250g / 9oz pack dried egg or wheat noodles

2 tablespoons cooking oil

125g / 4oz fresh beansprouts

salt and freshly ground black pepper

1. Plunge the noodles into a large saucepan of boiling water and cook or leave to stand for the time given on the pack. Drain well.

2. Heat the oil in a wok or deep frying pan and stir-fry the noodles with the beansprouts for 1 minute.

3. Season and serve at once.

Variations

Optional flavourings include:

* 1 tablespoon soy sauce
* a few drops of sesame oil
* a pinch of five spice powder
* 1 teaspoon Thai red curry paste

Herby Noodles

Fresh herbs can turn a simple noodle dish into a feast. Use butter or oil depending on the base of the dish you will be serving with the noodles.

½ x 250g / 9oz pack dried egg or wheat noodles

2 tablespoons cooking oil, olive oil or butter

2 tablespoons freshly chopped mint

a little fresh thyme or marjoram

salt and freshly ground black pepper

1. Plunge the noodles into a large saucepan of boiling water and cook or leave to stand for the length of time given on the pack. Drain well.

2. Heat the oil or butter in a wok or deep frying pan and toss the noodles with the herbs and seasoning. Serve at once.

Variations

Good combinations of herbs include:

* Parsley, basil and thyme

* Oregano, rosemary and parsley

* Fennel and parsley

* Dill, parsley and garlic

Noodles
with
Peppers and Almonds

If you want a particularly colourful dish, use a mixture of red, green and yellow peppers. This dish makes a special occasion meal if you team it up with frozen Chinese crispy duck and another dish or two from the freezer or chiller cabinet.

3 tablespoons flaked almonds

½ x 250g / 9oz pack dried wholewheat noodles

2 tablespoons cooking oil

I red pepper, seeded and cut into strips

salt and freshly ground black pepper

1. Toast the almonds in a dry frying pan or under the grill, shaking or stirring them constantly to ensure that they do not burn.

2. Plunge the noodles into a large saucepan of boiling water and cook or leave to stand for the length of time given on the pack.

3. Heat the oil in a wok or deep-frying pan and stir-fry the peppers for a couple of minutes until soft. Drain the noodles well and add to the pan of peppers.

4. Toss over a medium heat with the toasted almonds. Season and serve at once.

Wiltshire
Noodles

A friend of mine grows masses of chives in her Wiltshire garden and this is one of her favourite ways of using up a crop. You could, of course, substitute whichever herb you may happen to have in abundance. Serve with grilled tofu, scrambled eggs or poached fish.

225g / 8oz fresh noodles

salt

2 tablespoons mayonnaise

3-4 tablespoons freshly chopped chives

plenty of freshly ground black pepper

1. Gradually add the noodles to a large saucepan of boiling salted water without allowing the water to go off the boil. Cook for 2-3 minutes until the noodles are just tender.

2. Drain very well and toss with all the remaining ingredients. Serve at once.

Orange and Sesame Noodles

I serve this delicious noodle dish as an accompaniment to grilled breast of duck but it also works well with chicken and lamb cutlets.

2 tablespoons sesame seeds

I orange

½ x 250g / 9oz pack dried egg noodles

I tablespoon cooking oil

salt and freshly ground black pepper

1. Toast the sesame seeds in a dry frying pan or under the grill. Stir or shake them constantly to ensure that they do not burn.

2. Grate the rind from the orange. Remove the rest of the peel, then divide the flesh into segments. Remove any seeds and chop the flesh.

3. Plunge the noodles into a large pan of boiling water and cook or leave to stand for the length of time given on the pack.

4. Drain the noodles and return to the pan. Add the oil, orange rind and chopped flesh, sesame seeds and seasoning, then toss over a medium heat. Serve at once.

Variation
* Add ½ bunch watercress, coarsely chopped.

Lebanese Noodles with Lentils

Lentils are a very important ingredient in Lebanese cooking. They are often served mixed with rice, but they are also combined with noodles and this recipe is said to pre-date Marco Polo and Italian pasta. It is very good served with lamb kebabs.

50g / 2oz whole lentils, washed

125g / 4oz dried wheat noodles

2 tablespoons olive oil

½ large onion, peeled and finely chopped

I clove garlic, peeled and finely chopped

salt and freshly ground black pepper

2 tablespoons freshly chopped coriander leaves

1. Cover the lentils with plenty of water and bring to the boil. Simmer for 20-25 minutes until just tender. Do not allow them to over-cook and go mushy.

2. Plunge the noodles into a large saucepan of boiling water and cook or leave to stand for the length of time given on the pack.

3. Heat the oil in another pan and fry the onion and garlic until they are golden brown. Add the drained lentils, seasoning and coriander and mix carefully together.

4. Drain the noodles and add to the lentil sauce. Toss carefully and serve at once.

Pake Noodles

Pake is the Hawaiian word for Chinese. The inspiration for this recipe comes from Hong Kong via Hawaii and Trader Vic's chain of restaurants in the US. Serve with exotic casseroles or a fruity Malay curry.

½ x 250g / 9oz pack dried egg noodles

25g / 1oz fresh breadcrumbs

1 tablespoon sesame seeds

25g / 1oz butter

salt

white pepper

1. Plunge the dried egg noodles into a saucepan of boiling water. Cook or leave to stand for the length of time given on the pack.

2. Toast the breadcrumbs under the grill or in a dry frying pan until well browned.

3. Next, toast the sesame seeds in the same way. These will brown much more quickly so shake or stir frequently to ensure that they do not burn.

4. Melt the butter in a deep pan. Drain and dry the noodles and toss in the butter.

5. Stir in the breadcrumbs, sesame seeds and seasoning. Toss and serve.

Variations

* Substitute sunflower seeds or shelled pumpkin seeds for the sesame seeds.

* Add freshly chopped herbs such as parsley, mint, basil or tarragon just before serving.

Chinese Rice Noodles

This is a westernised version of a Hong Kong recipe. It makes an unusual accompaniment to any kind of grill or barbecue.

I egg

50g / 2oz long grain rice

salt

50g / 2oz rice or cellophane noodles

I tablespoon cooking oil

I teaspoon soy sauce

I tablespoon freshly chopped chives

1. Hard boil the egg; peel and chop.

2. Bring 150ml / ¼ pint salted water to the boil in a saucepan and add the rice. Stir, cover with a lid and reduce the heat. Simmer for 12-13 minutes until all the liquid has been absorbed and the rice is cooked through. If there is any sign of water, continue cooking for a further minute or so.

3. Plunge the noodles into a large saucepan of boiling water and cook for the length of time given on the pack. Drain and toss in oil. Cut into shorter lengths.

4. Place the rice, noodles and chopped egg in a bowl and add the remaining ingredients. Toss lightly together and serve at once.

Italian Herby Noodles with Peas

This is a wonderful dish to serve in the spring when the first new lamb joints arrive in the shops. It is also very good with roast poussin, grilled fish or barbecued kebabs

125g / 4oz fresh or frozen peas

salt

225g /8oz fresh Italian noodles or tagliatelle

½ tablespoon olive oil

1 tablespoon freshly chopped basil

1 tablespoon freshly chopped parsley

½ tablespoon freshly chopped chives

a little crushed garlic to taste

freshly ground black pepper

1. Cook the peas in plenty of salted boiling water, until tender.

2. Gradually add the noodles to a pan of salted boiling water, taking care not to allow the water to go off the boil.

3. Drain both the peas and the noodles very well and toss together with the oil, herbs and seasoning and serve.

Egg Fried Noodles

This is my simplified version of an authentic Indonesian noodle dish. It can be served with almost any stir-fried dish.

2 tablespoons cooking oil

2 eggs, beaten

225g / 8oz dried egg noodles

I clove garlic, peeled and crushed

2 lumps stem ginger, finely chopped

I onion, peeled and finely chopped

2 sticks celery, finely sliced

I tablespoon soy sauce

2 tablespoons sherry

I bunch spring onions, trimmed and sliced lengthways

1. Heat 1 tablespoon of oil in a frying pan and pour in the beaten eggs. Allow the eggs to spread out to make a large flat omelette. When it is cooked through remove from the pan and cut into strips. Keep warm.

2. Plunge the noodles into a saucepan of boiling salted water and cook or leave to stand for the length of time given on the pack. Drain and keep on one side.

3. Heat the remaining oil in a large frying pan or wok and stir-fry the garlic, ginger, onion and celery for about 5-8 minutes until tender.

4. Drain the noodles and add to the pan of stir-fried vegetables with the soy sauce and sherry. Heat through, stirring well to distribute the sauce among the noodles.

5. Serve garnished with slices of spring onion and the omelette strips.

Spicy Citrus Noodles

The wonderfully fruity flavours of this unusual noodle dish are typical of the new wave of Californian cooking. The dish adds lots of interest to plain grills but it makes an equally good match for the stronger flavours of ready-prepared barbecued spare-ribs or chicken tikka.

3 tablespoons sesame seeds

1 orange

1 lemon

1 tablespoon soy sauce

few drops of Tabasco sauce

½ x 250g / 9oz pack of dried egg noodles

1 tablespoon cooking oil

1 teaspoon oriental roasted sesame oil

2 cloves garlic, peeled and chopped

4-6 spring onions, trimmed and sliced

1. Toast the sesame seeds under the grill or in a dry frying pan over a medium heat, stirring them constantly to ensure that they do not burn.

2. Pare thin strips of peel off both fruit with a zester or sharp knife and if necessary cut into thinner strips. Cut the fruit in half, squeeze out the juice and strain.

3. Mix half the zest and all the juice with the soy sauce and Tabasco and keep on one side.

4. Plunge the dried egg noodles into a saucepan of boiling water. Cook or leave to stand for the length of time given on the pack.

5. Heat both the oils in a small pan and fry the garlic and spring onions for 1 minute. Add the juice mixture. Bring to the boil and cook over a high heat for about 3-4 minutes to reduce the mixture by about half.

6. Drain the noodles well and pour the sauce over the top. Add most of the toasted sesame seeds. Toss and turn into a serving dish. Top with remaining zest and sesame seeds and serve.

NOODLE
SALADS

Rather surprisingly, noodles can taste just as good cold as when they are hot as I found when I ordered a simple dish of Japanese Noodles at Matsuri restaurant in London. The cold noodles were served with a little seaweed and a wonderful dressing of soy sauce, miso and fish stock.

I started by using up leftover noodles in salads of various kinds and ended up cooking noodles specifically for the salads.

A noodle salad makes an attractive and substantial accompaniment to grills, roasts and barbecues. It can also form the basis of a summer meal or lunch snack.

The best noodles to use for salads are egg, wheat or buckwheat noodles. Rice and bean based noodles tend to be much sticker when they are cold and are therefore more difficult to deal with. Other types of noodles may also start to stick together as they cool.

The way to avoid noodles sticking together is to toss them in a little oil, or indeed the full salad dressing, whilst they are still hot after draining. Leave to cool and use as required.

Italian
Fresh Noodle Salad
with Vegetables

This colourful salad makes an excellent accompaniment to grilled hamburgers or barbecued sausages.

40-50g / 1½-2oz dried egg noodles or 75-125g / 3-4oz fresh Italian noodles, cut into shorter lengths

salt

1 tablespoon vegetable oil

½ teaspoon cider or wine vinegar

1 cooked beetroot, peeled and diced

2 sticks celery, finely sliced

1 carrot, coarsely grated

3 tablespoons mayonnaise

salt and freshly ground black pepper

1. If using dried egg noodles, plunge the noodles into a saucepan of boiling water and cook or leave to stand for the length of time given on the pack. If using fresh Italian noodles, cook the noodles in plenty of boiling salted water for about 2-3 minutes until just tender. Drain well and turn into a bowl. Toss with the oil and vinegar.

2. Place the vegetables in a serving bowl and toss with the mayonnaise.

3. Fold the noodles into the vegetable and mayonnaise mixture and season to taste. Keep in the fridge until required.

Variation
* To make a more substantial main course salad add a 200g / 7oz can of drained and flaked tuna, perhaps with a few chopped walnut halves.

Cold Tossed Noodles
with
Cucumber Sesame Sauce

I particularly like this well flavoured salad with grilled or fried chicken pieces. Cook your own, or buy a take-away.

I tablespoon sesame seeds

2 tablespoons salad oil

I teaspoon oriental roasted sesame oil

I teaspoon herb vinegar

salt and freshly ground black pepper

125g / 4oz cold cooked noodles, cut into 1½in lengths

5cm / 2in length cucumber, diced or cut into thin sticks

sprigs of fresh herbs to match the vinegar

1. Toast the sesame seeds under the grill or in a dry frying pan, stirring or shaking frequently to ensure that they do not burn.

2. Pour the two oils and the vinegar into a cup. Add the seasoning and whisk with a fork. Stir in the sesame seeds.

3. Pour the sesame dressing over the noodles, and toss. Add the cucumber sticks and toss again.

4. Spoon into a serving bowl and garnish with sprigs of herb that match the flavour of the vinegar used.

Variations

* You will achieve a less punchy and more nutty flavour if you use unrefined sesame oil in place of the mixture of oils given above.

* Substitute toasted sunflower seeds for sesame seeds for an even more nutty effect.

* In winter, when fresh herbs are not so easy to come by, substitute fresh herb-flavoured tagliatelle or fettucine.

Tossed Noodle Salad
with a Warm Dressing

I often serve this salad with poached fish and make extra dressing to act as an accompanying sauce.

75g / 3oz dried egg noodles

1 tablespoon salad oil

50g / 2oz Chinese beansprouts

50g / 2oz Chinese cabbage (leaves), shredded

¼ green pepper, seeded and finely shredded

½ red pepper, seeded and finely shredded

2.5cm / 1in piece cucumber, cut into thin sticks

1 carrot, coarsely grated

a little grated lemon rind

1 tablespoon lemon juice

2 tablespoons orange juice

1 teaspoon soy sauce

1. Plunge the noodles into a large saucepan of boiling water and cook or leave to stand for the length of time given on the pack. Drain well and toss in the oil.

2. Toss all the vegetables together in a bowl and add the noodles.

3. Place the grated lemon rind and lemon and orange juice in a small saucepan and bring to the boil. Stir in the soy sauce and pour over the salad.

4. Toss and serve at once.

Variation
* In the East, the salad mixture itself would be heated by very quickly stir-frying (for about 1 minute) in hot oil. Do this before Stage 2, taking care not to soften the vegetables too much.

Indonesian Noodle Salad
with Peanut Sauce

East meets West again with this salad inspired by the Indonesian Gado Gado salad. Serve with grilled lamb chops or with chicken or pork kebabs.

75g / 3oz thin wholemeal noodles

½ teaspoon oriental roasted sesame oil

2½ tablespoons salad oil

50g / 2oz salted dry roasted peanuts

I small clove garlic, peeled and chopped

**2 tablespoons light soy sauce or ordinary soy sauce
mixed with a little water**

2 teaspoons rice, cider or wine vinegar

125g / 4oz beansprouts

½ bunch watercress, coarsely chopped

4-6 radishes, sliced

5cm / 2in cucumber cut into sticks

1. Plunge the noodles into a large saucepan of boiling water and cook or leave to stand for the length of time given on the pack. Drain and dry, and chop roughly.

2. Mix the roasted sesame oil with half a tablespoon of salad oil and pour over the noodles. Toss well and leave to cool.

3. Place the remaining salad oil in a blender or food processor with the peanuts, garlic, soy sauce and vinegar. Process until smooth.

4. Toss the noodles with the beansprouts and other vegetables. Pour the peanut mixture over and toss well together.

Variation
* Add 1 fresh green chilli, with the seeds removed, to the peanuts for a hotter and more authentic flavour.

Prawn and Noodle Salad
with Hot Sesame Vinaigrette

This makes a very good main course salad to serve either on its own or as part of a cold buffet. Choose the type of prawns to suit your budget.

75g / 3oz dried egg or wheat noodles

mixed salad leaves (gem lettuces, lollo rosso, oakleaf and soft lettuce)

I small carrot, peeled and cut into thin sticks

I papaya, peeled, seeded and diced

175g / 6oz cooked peeled cocktail or king prawns

4 spring onions, trimmed and chopped

pared strips of lemon zest cut into thin sticks

sprigs of fresh chervil, parsley or dill

Sesame Vinaigrette:

3 tablespoons sunflower oil

2 teaspoons lemon juice

I teaspoon soy sauce

¼ teaspoon sesame seed oil

I tablespoon toasted sesame seeds

1. Plunge the noodles into a saucepan of boiling water and cook or leave to stand for the length of time directed on the pack.

2. Next make the vinaigrette by mixing all the ingredients together in a jug.

3. Drain the noodles and toss with a tablespoonful of the dressing while they are still warm. Leave to cool.

4. Tear the salad leaves into small pieces and mix with all the other salad ingredients. Pile into a large bowl and add the noodles and the rest of the dressing.

5. Toss well again and serve at once.

Crunchy Salsa
with
Deep Fried Noodles

The longer you can leave this refreshingly fresh and spicy Mexican-style salad to stand the better it will taste. You can even make it a day in advance. Serve any leftover salsa as a side dish to pep up grills or roasts later in the week.

In contrast, the crispy noodle base should be cooked at the very last minute. If you fry the noodles too soon they start to lose their crispness and go tough.

I small green pepper

I large English tomato or a small continental tomato

½ small onion, peeled and finely chopped

I fresh green chilli, seeded and finely chopped

2-4 tablespoons freshly chopped coriander

I tablespoon lemon juice

salt and freshly ground black pepper

75g / 3oz flat rice noodles

cooking oil

1. Prepare the pepper by removing the seeds and cutting the flesh into thin strips. Cut the strips into small cubes.

2. Cut the tomato in half and scoop out the seeds. Dice the flesh to the same size as the peppers.

3. Place the remaining ingredients, except the noodles and oil, in a serving bowl and toss well together. Leave to stand until required.

4. Fill a small saucepan about a third full of cooking oil. Heat the cooking oil until a piece of rice noodle dropped into the pan immediately swells to two or three times its original size and is crisp.

5. Add the whole 75g / 3oz bundle and keep under the fat with a slotted spoon. The noodles should swell up immediately. Wait for a minute or so to ensure that the noodles in the middle of the bundle have come into contact with the fat. Take care not to leave them too long and remove if they start to brown at all.

6. Drain the noodle bundle on kitchen paper and place on a serving plate. Spoon the previously prepared salsa over the top and serve at once.

Variations

* Give a European flavour to the salsa by using mild red onions with a clove of garlic in place of the ordinary onion and using fresh basil, dill or tarragon in place of coriander.

* Alternatively use red peppers instead of green and add some sweetcorn kernels for colour.

SWEET
NOODLE
DISHES

Before starting on this book I had enjoyed some really delicious sweet dishes made with noodles from both the Middle East and from India, so it was not too difficult to start thinking about Western ideas as well.

These recipes are all extremely quick to make, so if you are feeling particularly hungry and want a quickly prepared and filling finish to your meal - or you just have a sweet tooth – try them.

Hot Tossed Apricot
and
Almond Noodles

This has to be one of the easiest of desserts to make in a hurry. It's even quicker if you use dried egg noodles soaked for 5 minutes in boiling water.

50g / 2oz dried fettuccine or thin flat Italian noodles

2 tablespoons flaked almonds

3 tablespoons apricot jam

I teaspoon lemon juice

2-4 scoops vanilla ice-cream

1. Cook the noodles in plenty of lightly salted boiling water for 8-10 minutes until just cooked or for the length of time given on the pack.

2. Toast the flaked almonds under the grill or in a dry frying pan until they are well browned, taking care to keep them on the move so that they are evenly browned all over.

3. Spoon the jam into a saucepan with the lemon juice and place over a medium heat. Bring to the boil, stirring all the time. Cook for a minute or so, but do not allow the jam to get too thick or it will turn to toffee.

4. Drain the noodles and dry on kitchen paper. Add to the pan with the jam and toasted almonds and toss well together.

5. Serve at once on heated plates with ice cream.

Variations

* Seville orange marmalade with a dash of whisky.

* Pineapple jam with a dash of lime juice.

* Lemon curd with roasted pinenuts.

Egg Noodles
in
Chocolate Sauce

This is the recipe that I always use when I want a good chocolate sauce. It is quite rich and ice-cream can help to balance the dish.

50-75g / 2-3oz dried egg noodles

knob of butter

Chocolate Sauce:

50g / 2oz plain dessert chocolate

15g / ½oz butter

15g / ½oz cocoa

1 tablespoon golden syrup

1 tablespoon water

1. Plunge the noodles into a saucepan of boiling water and cook or leave to stand for the length of time given on the pack. Drain very well and toss with the knob of butter to keep the strands separate. Keep warm until required.

2. Meanwhile, make the sauce by melting the chocolate in a basin over a pan of hot water. Gradually stir in the butter, followed by the cocoa and then the golden syrup and water.

3. Pour the sauce over the hot noodles, toss and serve at once, with ice-cream if liked.

Indian Vermicelli Pudding

This unusual pudding can be served hot but it is also very good when it is cold. I often make double the quantity and spoon half into a small dish to store in the fridge. The mixture sets when it is cold and it makes a good sweet snack cut into slices or wedges.

40g / 1½oz unsalted butter

75g / 3oz dried Italian vermicelli

200ml / 8fl oz milk

125g / 4oz sugar

pinch of saffron

seeds from 2-3 cardamom pods, crushed

15g / ½oz flaked almonds

1. Heat the butter in a pan and fry the vermicelli until it is golden brown, taking care not to burn it.

2. Pour on the milk and bring to the boil. Cover and simmer for about 4-5 minutes until the vermicelli is soft, stirring from time to time.

3. Add the sugar, stir well and turn up the heat. Continue cooking, stirring all the time, until all the liquid has evaporated. Add the saffron, cardamom and almonds and serve.

Fresh Fruit
in
Crispy Noodle Nests

Leave the making of the noodle nests to the very last minute for they will lose their crispness very quickly.

50g / 2oz rice vermicelli

cooking oil

175g / 6oz fresh raspberries

1 tablespoon sugar

2 ripe peaches, stoned and chopped

1. To deep fry the vermicelli, heat the oil in a small but deep saucepan. The oil should come about a third of the way up the side of the pan. Drop a small piece of dry noodle into the fat to see if it is hot enough - it should puff up immediately.

2. When the fat is ready, drop a bundle of half the noodles into the fat. The noodles should puff up immediately, making a small nest the diameter of the pan. Remove with a perforated spoon and drain on kitchen paper. Repeat with the remaining bundle of noodles.

3. Rub 125g / 4oz of the raspberries through a sieve to make a coulis. Sweeten with the sugar.

4. Mix the remaining raspberries with the peaches and pile on top of each crispy noodle bundle. Pour the raspberry coulis over the top and serve at once.

Variations

* Use 2 bananas, or a mango, in place of the peaches.

* Substitute really ripe fresh blackberries for the raspberries and serve with apples, pears or pineapple.

Chocolate Noodles
with Pears and Ice-cream

A few delicatessen shops sell chocolate flavoured fresh pasta and this is fun to use in this recipe. However, if you cannot find any, simply make the Egg Noodles in Chocolate Sauce (recipe on page 132) and use instead.

125g / 4oz fresh chocolate noodles

knob of butter

2 pears, peeled and chopped

25g / 1oz plain dessert chocolate, grated

2-4 scoops vanilla ice-cream

1. Plunge the noodles into a large saucepan of boiling water and cook for 2-3 minutes until just tender. Drain well and toss in the knob of butter.

2. Next add the pears and chocolate and toss again.

3. Pile the noodles onto two plates and top with the ice-cream. Serve at once.

Noodles with Honey
and
Pistachio Nuts

This is my favourite noodle pudding. It has a real Middle Eastern flavour to it - and I can eat it by the bowlful!

50-75g / 2-3oz dried egg or wheat noodles

15g / ½oz butter

3 tablespoons pistachio nuts, finely chopped

¼ teaspoon ground cinnamon

seeds from 1 cardamom pod, crushed

2 tablespoons clear honey

1. Plunge the noodles into a large saucepan of boiling water and cook or leave to stand for the time given on the pack.

2. Heat the butter in a saucepan and gently fry the nuts. Do not allow the mixture to burn. Stir in the spices as the mixture cooks.

3. Drain the noodles very well and add to the pan of nuts. Pour on the honey and toss well together. Serve at once.

INDEX

Italian dried noodles, 10
  chicken cacciatore with, 63
  pasticcio, 101
  Italian noodles with bacon sauce, 69
Italian fresh noodle salad with vegetables, 121
Italian herby noodles with peas, 116

J

Japanese chicken ball soup with seasonal greens, 28-9
Japanese noodles, 11-12

K

kidneys:
  devilled kidneys with fresh noodles, 72
kintobi noodles, 11

L

Lebanese noodles with lentils, 113
lemon sole:
  Oriental seafood soup, 21
lentils, Lebanese noodles with, 113
liver:
  Delaware chicken livers with fresh noodles and sage, 50
  pasticcio, 101

M

McKenzie noodles, 56
meatballs:
  Oriental meatballs with Chinese noodles, 70
mie noodles, 10
miso soup with tofu and cellophane noodles, 30
mushrooms: mixed mushroom soup with noodles, 24

N

Neapolitan sauce for fresh noodles, 53

O

olives, souffléd tomato noodles with, 103
oranges:
  orange and cardamom chicken wings on fresh noodles, 71
  orange and sesame noodles, 112
  spicy citrus noodles, 118
Oriental meatballs with Chinese noodles, 70
Oriental seafood soup, 21

P

pad thai noodles, 12
pake noodles, 114
pancakes: noodle pancakes with Florentine eggs, 84-5
pasticcio, 101
peaches:
  fresh fruit in crispy noodle nests, 134
peanut butter: egg noodles with Indonesian sauce, 46-7
peanut sauce, Indonesian noodle salad with, 124
pears, chocolate noodles with ice-cream and, 135
peas:
  fresh noodles with Boursin and peas, 41
  Italian herby noodles with, 116
peppers:
  noodles with almonds and, 110
  pepper noodles with ham, 59
  piperade with fresh noodles, 67
  pork and pepper stir-fry with Chinese noodles, 54
pesto soup with noodles, 25
piperade with fresh noodles, 67
pistachio nuts, noodles with honey and, 136
plaice: teriyaki plaice with egg noodles, 66
pork:
  crunchy fried rice sticks with stir-fried pork, 88-9

BESTSELLING COOKBOOKS
FROM VERMILION

Dinner for a Fiver	*Nicholas Lander*	£4.99
Cosmopolitan After-Work Cookbook	*Richard Ehrlich*	£6.99
Loyd Grossman's Italian Journey	*Loyd Grossman*	£7.99
MasterChef 1994	*Loyd Grossman*	£8.99
Oxfam Vegetarian Cookbook	*Rose Elliot*	£8.99
New Pauper's Cookbook	*Jocasta Innes*	£8.99
Mediterranean Olive Oil Cookbook	*Louise Steele*	£9.99
Anton Mosimann – Naturally	*Anton Mosimann*	£9.99

Prices and other details are liable to change

Vermilion, Bookservice by Post, PO Box 29, Douglas, Isle Of Man, British Isles

Name _____

Address _____

_____

_____

_____

Please enclose a cheque or postal order made out to B.S.B.P Ltd, for the amount due and allow for the following for postage and packaging.

UK CUSTOMERS: Please allow 75p per book to a maximum order of £7.50.
B.F.P.O. & EIRE: Please allow 75p per book to a maximum of £7.50.
OVERSEAS CUSTOMERS: Please allow £1.00 per book.

Whilst every effort is made to keep prices low it is sometimes necessary to increase cover prices at short notice, Vermilion reserves the right to show new retail prices on covers which may differ from those previously advertised in the text or elsewhere.